PERSONAL FINANCE for PROFESSIONALS

Susan A. Berson

Cover design by Jill Tedhams/ABA Publishing.

Printed in the United States of America.

19 18 17 16 15 5 4 3 2 1

ISBN: 978-1-62722-759-9

e-ISBN: 978-1-62722-760-5

**Library of Congress Cataloging-in-Publication Data
is on file with the Library of Congress**

Discounts are available for books ordered in bulk. Special consideration is given to state bars, CLE programs, and other bar-related organizations. Inquire at Book Publishing, ABA Publishing, American Bar Association, 321 N. Clark Street, Chicago, Illinois 60654-7598.

www.ShopABA.org

Dedicated to those who are prosperous in spirit, may you soon have the portfolio to match.

Contents

About the Author

Susan began her legal career in Washington, D.C., in 1990, as a trial attorney at the United States Department of Justice, Tax Division, representing the Internal Revenue Service. While at the Justice Department, Susan received the Attorney General's Outstanding Attorney Award in 1996 for her legal work. In 1998, Susan entered private practice, relocating to Kansas City and becoming a Partner with an Am Law 100 law firm's business litigation practice group representing a broad client base ranging from *Fortune* 500 companies to small businesses in a variety of industries. In 2005, Susan founded her own law firm, focusing her practice on representing small-business owners involved in IRS and state tax disputes. Then, in 2007, she and her husband, Dave, an experienced banking and securities attorney, successfully integrated their practices into what is now known as the Berson Law Group LLP (www.banktaxlaw.com). Their firm primarily represents banks and small-business owners and their directors and officers. Every year since 2005, both Susan and Dave have been included in the "Best of the Bar" published by the *Business Journal* of Kansas City. Susan is admitted in the District of Columbia, Missouri, Kansas, the Courts of Appeals for the Sixth, Eighth, and Tenth Circuits, the U.S. Tax Court, the U.S. Court of Federal Claims, and the U.S. Supreme Court. A certified mediator, Susan is also retained by other attorneys to help their clients find cost-effective resolutions to problems and disputes. She also presides over administrative hearings involving financial professionals and their clients as a FINRA Arbitrator.

In addition to her law practice, Susan is a contributing columnist for the *ABA Journal Magazine*'s retirement series; author of the treatise *Federal Tax Litigation* (Law Journal Press, 2001, updated twice a year), *The Modern Rules of Personal Finance for Professionals* (American Bar Association, rev. 2014), and *The Lawyer's Retirement Planning Guide* (American Bar Association, rev. 2014); and coauthor of *The Dodd-Frank Wall Street Reform and Consumer Protection Act: From Legislation to Implementation to Litigation* (American Bar Association, 2011). A sought-after speaker, Susan teaches at conferences, seminars, and law firms on topics ranging from contingency planning for attorneys to personal finance to substantive legal issues involved in defending clients against the IRS and handling administrative hearings against government agencies.

Susan is a member of, and has held leadership positions in, several professional and civic associations, including the American Bar Association (ABA), the Kansas Women Attorneys Association, and the International Women's Insolvency & Restructuring Confederation (IWIRC), Midwest Region. Susan is especially active in Food from the Bar, originally a grassroots campaign by the National Conference of Women's Bar Associations to organize legal communities to raise food and monetary donations for their respective local pantries helping to feed the hungry.

Susan can be contacted at sberson@banktaxlaw.com.

A portion of the graphics provided by Brian J. Laughlin

Introduction

Financially speaking, most young professionals feel either smothered by student loan and credit card debt or euphoric at being flush with cash from a hefty paycheck and preparing to engage in mass consumerism and purchase all the accoutrements of wealth their hard work deserves. There are even a few who feel fortunate at being already financially wealthy—though not super-rich yet. No matter where you stand on this spectrum, this book is for you. Common to everyone is the often-quoted axiom, "People don't plan to fail, they fail to plan." That's true with financial success. By the way, the fly-by-the-seat-of-your-pants attitude, vowing to save next year, is not a plan. It eventually leads to financial problems, regardless of whether you're earning $60,000 or $1 million. When you become financially strapped, work—no matter how glamorous or prestigious—can seem more like a dungeon than a career.

The purpose of this book is to help you learn how to manage what you can control: your money. Effective money management is the tool that is going to help you find the means to achieve your dreams. After graduation, you begin at the helm of a glorious ship that's sailing off into a very beautiful sunset—but it's very important that you know what route you're going to follow. The advice in this book is based on the experiences of those who have sailed these waters before. The ideas offered could guarantee you a financially successful voyage. But, it depends on you. Will you work to fund a financial lifestyle or create financial independence? The price for financial independence can be as little as 10 percent of your paycheck every month. For those who are drowning in debt and feel as though they'll never get afloat, don't be discouraged. Remember that part of success is believing that you can do anything you set your mind to do—think of the billions amassed by Oprah Winfrey, Robert Redford, and Warren Buffett. Sure, your inner monologue says, they're all unique, but that only explains *why* they made money, not *how* they were able to retain and grow their wealth when others in their respective industries have lost or squandered their earnings. Armed with the sound financial practices in this book, achieving your financial goals will become milestones, not endpoints. There is a *multi*millionaire inside you—it just requires learning to effectively manage your spending and saving habits, as well as risk and contingency planning.

Chapter 1

Financial Goals: From Debt Free to Retiring Early

Without goals, and plans to reach them, you are like a ship that has set sail with no destination.

—Fitzhugh Dodson

When it comes to finances, it's important to be the captain of your own ship. Many professionals set career goals for themselves to achieve, yet put little energy into charting their financial goals. Where you are in life's events will dictate what you need and want and, thus, what your financial goals should be. For example, the number one priority of most recent graduates may be paying off their student loans. Seasoned working professionals, on the other hand, might be more interested in retiring early. Surprisingly, very few professionals, young or seasoned, take the time to chart out the financial goals that crop up when life events occur between becoming debt-free and retiring early. When it comes to your finances, winging it will not produce a positive result. Diagramming your financial goals, and a corresponding plan to achieve them, is key to achieving lifelong financial prosperity.

Drafting a blueprint for your financial prosperity involves three steps: (1) assessing your present financial condition, (2) determining your financial goals, and (3) developing a strategy to meet your goals. So, before doing anything else, assess where you are financially in life by preparing a balance sheet. List everything you own on one side of the page and all debt on the other side. Then, add up each side of the page, and subtract all of your liabilities from your total assets to arrive at your net worth. The Net Worth Balance Worksheet in Figure 1.1 can help you.

FIGURE 1.1
NET WORTH BALANCE WORKSHEET

LIABILITIES (WHAT YOU OWE)

Home mortgage/other real estate loans (balance owed) .... ________

Credit cards (balance owed on monthly credit card statement(s)) .... ________

Installment credit contract(s)—remaining balance on following:

- Auto .... ________
- Furniture or appliances .. ________
- Mobile home .... ________
- Home improvement .... ________
- Other .... ________
- Cash loans (balance owed) ________
- Taxes due .... ________
- Income .... ________
- Property .... ________
- Loans against insurance policies........... ________
- Notes payable .... ________

TOTAL LIABILITIES .... $ ________

Total Assets ________ $ ________

minus

Total Liabilities ________ $________

Total Net Worth ________ $________

ASSETS (WHAT YOU OWN THAT HAS VALUE)

Liquid assets .... ________

Cash in your wallet .... ________

Checking account .... ________

Money market account ..... ________

Savings account .... ________

Savings bonds .... ________

Certificates of deposit....... ________

Life insurance cash value .. ________

Securities (today's value) ... ________

Stocks .... ________

Mutual funds .... ________

Bond certificates............... ________

Other investments .... ________

Annuities .... ________

Tax shelters .... ________

IRA/Retirement .... ________

Personal property (resale value)..................... ________

Car .... ________

Motorcycle .... ________

Bicycle .... ________

Other vehicle .... ________

Household furniture .... ________

Antiques .... ________

Furs, jewelry, silver .... ________

Hobby equipment .... ________

Art, collectibles .... ________

Loan receivables owed to you .... ________

Real property .... ________

Home/Condo .... ________

Other .... ________

TOTAL ASSETS...............$ ________

Your total assets and liabilities should be reviewed annually to track your progress and gain an accurate understanding of your financial condition, should refining your priorities and goals become necessary.

FINANCIAL GOALS SHOULD TRACK PRIORITIES AND REALITY

The next step is to determine what your financial goals are. If you're like most up-and-coming professionals, the net worth calculation will reveal that your liabilities exceed your assets. If this is true, then your financial goals should include tackling that debt as well as building cash reserves and a retirement nest egg. That's before you buy the BMW, the Porsche, or the McMansion. Yes, you deserve these things, but believe this: five years from now, you will be better off financially and emotionally if you focus on paying off the debt, building your cash reserves, and establishing a retirement account before you spend to make yourself feel better. Indulgent spending will do little for your financial future and cause undue stress and anxiety, if not now, certainly later. That being said, your age, health, family responsibilities, and lifestyle will all play a role in determining what your financial wants and needs are. To help you get started, consider prioritizing the following:

___ Paying off school debts
___ Paying off credit cards
___ Emergency savings account (equal to six months of paychecks)
___ Insurance
___ Owning a car
___ Owning a home
___ Retirement
___ Vacation
___ Children
___ Elder care

This list is just a sampling of the common goals many professionals would consider relevant in their lives. You may have more, but this list is a starting point to help you prioritize what's important to accomplish over your income-producing years. Goals can be short term, such as buying a new suit next week, or medium term, such as paying off credit card debt, or long term, such as saving for retirement.

Here are age-appropriate goals for most young professionals to consider focusing on:

20s	30s	40s
(1) Pay off school loans, credit card and car loan debts	(1) Home Savings	(1) Investment
(2) Establish Emergency Savings	(2) Domestic Life/Family	(2) Job Changes
(3) Maximize Annual Retirement Contributions	(3) Job Changes	(3) Family/Elder Care
	(4) Continue to Maximize Annual Retirement Contributions	(4) Continue to Maximize Annual Retirement Contributions
		(5) Education

> Goals are personal, so decide what *you* want, as opposed to what someone wants for you. If you have a significant other or children, discuss your goals and priorities as a family. This discussion will be helpful later should your budget dictate that everyone must make temporary or permanent sacrifices to achieve your family's financial goals.

Regardless of age, there are three general rules to follow while working to achieve your goals.

1. **Achieve and Maintain a Debt-Free Existence:** There are many lenders who will always be willing to provide you with enough money for the lifestyle you want. However, they will charge a fee for this—a fee that can be better put to use growing your savings account or funding one of your goals. Paying off debt, particularly consumer debt, is the best way to build wealth in the long run.
2. **Establish an Emergency Fund:** An often ignored yet crucial category is the emergency fund. You should have cash set aside equal to six months' pay, though the ideal in a transitioning job market is 12 months. This is because the unexpected happens, and it often comes with a big price tag. If you don't have an emergency fund established for the curveballs of life, you'll

have to go (deeper) into debt. For example, car accidents with uninsured motorists, injuries in a softball game, family illness, or even being fired or laid off—all of these catastrophes commonly occur. You need a safety net so that when these unforeseen events happen, they don't thrust you into a deep (or deeper) financial hole.

> Sixty-eight percent of Americans have zero savings earmarked for emergencies.
> Source: U.S. Federal Reserve Board, Survey of Consumer Finance

3. **Max Out Annual Retirement Contributions:** Money set aside for retirement in a tax-deferred account is not taxed until retirement. Importantly, if your employer offers a retirement matching program, you should participate. By not participating, you are in essence giving up free money.

> The importance of starting retirement savings early, even with just a small amount, is demonstrated by this example. Assume a 25-year-old wants to live off 80 percent of a $43,000 salary (that is, $34,400 in retirement). Earning a conservative 4 percent rate of return on investments, this 25-year-old would have to save 12 percent of his or her salary annually to retire at 67 years old. Waiting until 45 to start saving would require a 31 percent annual savings rate on a $43,000 salary to accomplish retiring at 67 years old.
> Source: Boston College's Center for Retirement Research estimator

Once you have implemented these three rules, begin building your wealth by focusing on investments as well as buying the homes, cars, clothes, and other accoutrements of wealth. Obviously, you must tailor these three rules to your particular situation. For example, if you have an emergency savings fund already established and no credit card debt, whether to enter the investment world (beyond the maximum retirement contribution) depends on the interest rate and manageability of the student loan debt. If the student loan debt payment (discussed in Chapter 3) is a manageable $90, at an interest rate of 4 percent, it may be appropriate to consider investing (discussed in Chapter 7) or saving for a home (discussed in Chapter 5) instead of paying off the student loan debt early.

I WANT THAT! DISTINGUISHING BETWEEN WANT AND NEED

Distinguishing between a "want" and a "need" is critical to achieving your financial goals. You may want ten new power suits for your job, but you can get by with fewer, and with some employers, without any of them. Your monthly income and expenses will dictate whether to buy ten, five, or none, as discussed in Chapter 2.

EXPECTATION VERSUS REALITY

When determining financial goals, set aside the expectations you may have had in school. Slogging over the studies, it's common for the mind to cook up big ideas with big outcomes, envisioning the fancy car, spiffy clothing, and sleekly furnished home you'll have when you finally graduate and begin your career. If you promised you would reward yourself with a new BMW with that first paycheck, yet you haven't paid off your debt, funded an emergency savings account, and maxed out your retirement contribution for the year, it's best for your financial reality to postpone the fulfillment of that promise. It doesn't necessarily mean you're unable to buy a car for transportation needs, just not a $50,000 model. Before caving in to the expectations you had about a lawyer's life post-graduation (or others' expectations about what a lawyer's paycheck should get you or them), ask yourself this question: Am I willing to keep my legs pumping on the work treadmill for an extra five to ten years to indulge those expectations? For many, once they are actually on the job, the answer may be no.

> Nicki graduated from the Ivy League straight to an elite law firm, debt-ridden with $82,000 worth of student loans. Pampering her expensive tastes, and showing off her success with designer clothes, a modern apartment, and an expensive convertible, was a reward for all her efforts and sacrifices made during seven years of school. Unfortunately, after two years of billing 80-hour weeks and concealing the dark circles under her eyes, she wanted out. After selling the car, getting a roommate, and forgoing shopping sprees, she was still trapped in her job because of debt. She had to toil for another three and a half years to pay it off. Securing a good financial footing paved her exit to a serendipitous job at a start-up.

JOB SECURITY

Priorities may fluctuate with the stability of your employment. Although you likely excelled in school, you may have yet to really prove yourself with your new employer. Not to place extra pressure on you or turn up the flames of competition for advancement or partnership, but one well-written memo on collateral estoppel is not proving yourself. You prove yourself by demonstrating value. It can take up to three years before you, as a worker, are truly profitable to your employer. Essentially, most lawyers learn the law (it is hoped) in law school and spend the first four to five years of their career learning how to practice law. Whether it's developing and trying a case, handling a merger, or dealing favorably with clients, until you have a day-to-day mastering of those skills, don't get too comfortable. This means some at your new employer may remain wary of you, and that translates to job insecurity. As a matter of fact, for many firms, it isn't until associates pass the five-year anniversary that a significant profit will actually have been made from the training that has been invested in them. (The five-year anniversary is also when many young lawyers can predict whether their future lies with the firm.)

Also, corporate bankruptcies and downsizing, law firm mergers, and rainmaking partners' exits can put even a go-to attorney's job in jeopardy. No matter how smart or skilled a lawyer may be, if client work in a particular practice group dries up because of the economy, conflicts with a merging firm, or a partner's departure, an employer simply can't afford to keep an associate on when there is nothing to bill (no matter how profitable other areas in the firm are). Even plaintiffs' firms are not immune. Think of "King of Torts" Melvin Belli's firm filing for bankruptcy protection in 1995 after Dow Corning declared bankruptcy, leaving Belli with no way to recover the $5,000,000+ he owed to experts and others who helped him in the plaintiffs' suit he had won against Dow. For many young professionals, their employers will operate a treadmill paved with gold. Nevertheless, remain conscious of the potential for a slowdown; otherwise, your financial climb will become much more difficult without financial contingency preparation.

Chapter 2

The "B" Word: Everyone Needs a Budget

The amount of money you have has got nothing to do with what you earn. People earning a million dollars a year can have no money and people earning $35,000 a year can be quite well off. It's not what you earn, it's what you spend.

—Paul Clitheroe

A budget is your playbook for how you'll be spending and saving your money. Everyone needs one. Budgets need not involve clipping coupons or instituting austere measures. In fact, the secret of most millionaires is that they live on a budget. Yes, a multimillionaire's budget may allow for large discretionary income purchases, but she or he doesn't spend money on something unless it is within the budgeted category or item. Why? Because a budget helps to guide you toward your goals.

Before you can prepare your plan for what you'll spend on and how much you'll spend, you have to determine where your money has been going so that you can set realistic goals for your spending habits. If you haven't been keeping records concerning your spending and saving habits, now is the time to start. For the next month, record all checks, credit card charges, and ATM withdrawals to track your expenses. An organized record-keeping system is a must for budgeting and financial success. Your record keeping can be as simple as putting pen to paper and creating a financial diary/journal, or it can be computerized. The computer-generated record keepers are preferred by most because they also provide a financial analysis that summarizes expenses based on the information you supply, with a recommendation of the steps to take to achieve saving strategies. There are a number of software programs on the market, Quicken being one of the best selling and most user-friendly. It has several features you may never use, but it is good for automatically reconciling bank statements, tracking expenses, budgeting, and gathering information for tax time. An important feature allows you to print reports and easily compare what you're actually spending and saving with your budgeted financial goals.

Nevertheless, even if you purchase a computer program to track your finances, you ought to do a first draft of your own with a legal pad and pencil. Either way, when developing your plan, it's not important how it looks, just that the system works and you use it. It must be customized according to how you live.

PAGE ONE: ADD UP YOUR ANNUAL INCOME

For most people, this is a short list consisting of your net monthly pay (after taxes are deducted from your paycheck). However, if you're fortunate to have additional income, such as a trust fund, dividends, or sales of paintings created in your spare time, list it, too. Do not include year-end bonuses or raises unless you have actually been paid these amounts. The purpose of this exercise is to determine what the average monthly income you have to allocate will be.

PAGE TWO: COLUMN A—LIST ALL CATEGORIES OF EXPENSES

Rent, mortgage, gas, and charity are examples of the categories to include. In naming your categories, be as broad or specific as you want, whatever method works for you. For example, "Entertainment" can be all-encompassing, including everything from dinners to DVD rentals to baseball tickets and bar tabs, or you can list every specific event or activity as a subcategory of Entertainment. The important thing is that if you spend money on it, you list it. If you have a 20-dollar co-pay for your semiannual routine dental appointment, list it. Other annual expenditures, such as auto insurance, should also be listed, but calculated on a monthly basis. For example, if your car insurance is $900 a year, divide that amount by 12—the result is $75. Also, if you own a car, include a category for maintenance costs. Similarly, if you own a condo or home, make sure to include a maintenance and repairs category. Though what may need fixing cannot always be anticipated, it is wise to set aside a certain amount per month. For example, if you've been told the roof will need replacing in four years, do not budget $0 for the first three years and then $12,000 for the last year. Allocate $3,000 for each year and break it down even further to 12 monthly payments (of $250) to save up for that new roof.

Importantly, credit cards should not be listed as a category except for the annual fee, if any. On the other hand, items you charge on the credit card, such as clothing, furniture, restaurant meals, travel, and the like, are categories to include on your list. As a guide, consider the sample categories listed in the following chart.

Weekly Expenses	Monthly Expenses	Quarterly/Annual Expenses
Food, Transportation	Rent/Mortgage, Utilities	Insurance, Taxes
Household Supplies	Phone, Loan Payments	Repairs, Clothing, Charity
Entertainment	Savings/Investment	Pet Vaccinations, Licenses
Dry Cleaning	Medical/Dental/Health Care	Hair Stylist/Barber

After listing all categories of expenses, take another stab at it. Review the list and make certain there is nothing you have left out—your afternoon Starbuck's, Friday Happy Hour, iTunes downloads, pet toys, tailoring—inevitably, there is something you have forgotten. Remember to include items that are not always consistent, such as birthday and holiday gifts, unreimbursed association fees, and the like. To get an idea of what you spend, consider reviewing any records (bills, credit card statements, receipts) you've kept from last year. If you don't have records to re-create your expenses, carry a notebook for the next month and jot down all of your income and expenses, from gassing up your car to DVD rentals. For the items that are yearly costs, divide by 12 for an average monthly expenditure.

When you make ATM withdrawals, it's important to track where this cash goes, too. Record keeping can be time-consuming, but it is often the cash withdrawals that are most susceptible to slipping through your hands.

> **Taking Inventory**: If you're not a detail-oriented person or if you consider tracking every purchase too time-consuming and tedious, consider this for encouragement: one morning Starbuck's Venti adds up to $400 per year; a weekly bottle of wine can be $650 annually; and a pack-a-day cigarette habit, $1,700 per year. Assume you quit the habit and begin investing the monthly cigarette money, at a 5 percent interest rate, when you are 25 years old. By the age of 65, you will have earned over $325,000. Tracking all your expenses now will make it easier to figure out ways to make adjustments and save even more. Small amounts add up, so keep track!

Next, analyze your monthly income and monthly expenses. If the total income figure is higher than expenses, you have a net positive cash flow that can be used, along with any funds you have already saved, to invest, buy a home, and further your goals. If your expenses are higher than your income, however, you will need to reduce your expenses or increase your income to achieve a positive cash flow.

PAGE TWO: COLUMN B—COST-SAVING ADJUSTMENTS

Once you've established how much you have available and where your money is going, the next step is to find ways to reduce spending and free up more cash for saving or putting toward your other goals. To the extent you have discretionary spending, this is usually the easiest category to start with. The idea is not to deprive yourself but to channel money toward the goals that are important to you. For some, there may not be much fat in the budget to cut. It may become necessary to make lifestyle changes. For example, smoking is an expensive habit. If you've thought of quitting, now's the time to try and funnel that pack-a-day habit into a goal that is important to you. Do you have expensive hobbies, interests, or vices you can limit or eliminate? Ask yourself some tough questions about your lifestyle and interests and how they mesh with your financial goals. The following are some tips for saving money to jump-start your brainstorming session.

Car and Maintenance: If you live in a city with readily available public transportation, ask yourself whether you can do without a car for a few years (and its gas, insurance, maintenance, and loan payments), or whether you can at least curtail its use and redirect the money you spend on gas to another goal. Should you decide the cost of car ownership is worth the use/pleasure you receive from it, consider whether you can get by with a less expensive vehicle (e.g., a BMW versus a Honda Civic). If so, calculate whether the profit from selling it and buying a cheaper model will help you achieve your financial goals sooner.

Auto Insurance: Consider your deductible needs and the likelihood of having an accident versus paying a higher deductible. Similarly, depending on the age of your vehicle, consider whether dropping collision coverage and retaining liability coverage is financially better for you. For example, a driver with a good driving record who owns a ten-year-old car may be financially better off paying a $500 deductible instead of $250 and dropping the collision coverage on a car that is likely worth only a few thousand dollars.

Housing: The general rule to follow is that housing costs should not exceed one-fourth of take-home pay; however, some regions (e.g., New York City, San Francisco) can have skyrocketing housing markets that make it difficult to follow this rule. If your rent is significantly higher because of the market you're in, consider whether to take in a roommate—even if only for a year—and put that rental income toward your financial goals. Utilities, telephone, cable, and Internet are common expenses whether you rent or own. If you own, remember to include property taxes in the mix. If the going gets really tough, consider whether you can live without cable or lunches or dinners out for a while. Find ways to plug the drain on your paycheck, if not permanently, at least temporarily.

Phone Service: With respect to cellular phone service, make certain that your plan actually matches the minutes you use. Overpaying can add up. If you have a cellular phone and a landline, consider whether you really need both. Also, if you decide to retain a landline, long distance carriers continually alter their plans. Consider reviewing whether you can save money with your long distance carrier. Also, block international calling on your cell service—unless you need it—to deter fraudulent charges.

Entertainment: This category is usually the easiest to target for cutbacks, though the items can be the most mentally difficult to part with. Cover charges to bars/clubs, gourmet coffee drinks, movies, concerts, sporting events, poker night, art exhibitions, golf, subscriptions—if you can forgo some of these activities for a while, financially you will have more to gain in furthering your goals. For example, spending 30 to 40 percent of your paycheck on entertainment is grossly out of line with your goals when you are nursing credit card debt.

Banking: Consider whether the fees, if any, you are paying for your accounts are really worth it. If you keep a low minimum balance in your checking account, consider switching to a bank with no minimum balance and no fees. If you're a debit card user, research banks that offer a "keep the change" program. In it, purchases are rounded up to the nearest dollar, and the difference can be deposited in your savings account.

Servicing Your Debt: Go over the list of everything you owe money on—car, student loans, credit cards, overdraft protection—and then determine the interest rate that you are paying on your loans, including credit cards, breaking down the principal and interest portion of your payments. Generally, if more than 36 percent of your income is servicing high-interest debts, you must schedule these in your goals for pay-off. Also, consider researching the credit cards offered by the organizations you have membership in. Some may offer a credit card with a lower interest rate (and lower annual fee). By the way, if paying off that debt is not one of your goals, reconsider with this fact in mind: paying interest takes money that could be better directed to reaching your own goals than to making your lender rich. Chapters 3 and 4 will discuss, in detail, targeting student loan and credit card debts. For those who are used to spending more than they earn, this course could become painful. If you start to crumble, just remember the interest portion of your payments could be funding financial goals that are important to you.

Classifieds and eBay: Do you have unused items you have been storing for years (e.g., clothes, furniture, musical instruments) that can be sold for cash?

Avoid Retail Therapy: Shopping for comfort or recreation is not conducive to accomplishing your financial goals. When you shop—whether for groceries, clothes, electronics, single malt scotch, or a car—decide how much you have available to spend before you ever go online or step foot in the store. With a plan for spending, you should be questioning whether you really "need" that item. If you can achieve your financial goals without it, chances are you don't "need" it, you just "want" it. Don't deprive yourself of things you really need, but don't give in to impulse spending to make you momentarily feel good either.

Gift Giving: Financial commitments to nonprofit or religious organizations, your alma mater, social services agencies, or the arts, plus gifts at birthdays, weddings, baby showers, office celebrations, and holidays—they all add up. When creating a budget, allocate money for giving every month because you know you're going to need it. When the time to buy birthday or holiday presents actually arrives, it won't bust your budget. Consider picking up presents during sales year-round; last-minute shopping is when retailers can charge top dollar. You need not be a Scrooge during the holidays, but you don't want to wake to a hangover when the partying is over either. Overspending for most Americans occurs in December. To stay on track, just as you do for your own goals, make a list of people for whom you must purchase gifts and allocate a limit for each person.

The preceding are only a few suggestions. Take the time to review your expenses in Column A and consider what expenditures, if any, you can do without and which ones can be tweaked for extra savings. The goal of this exercise is to develop information for a budget. The budget is going to be used to manage your cash flow so you can pay your present expenses and still meet your lifelong goals. You'll likely need to adjust your expenses to cover immediate needs and still achieve your short-term and long-term goals. Putting a temporary embargo on new purchases until the emergency savings account is built up is one example. Careful scrutiny of your personal habits and spending will likely identify more. Record all of them in Column B. Find cost-cutting ideas at http://www.stretcher.com or ways to save at http://www.bills.com/ways-to-save/. Considering a relocation for a reduced cost of living? Estimate relocation savings at http://basic.esplanner.com/.

> "I'd be willing to take your pen and jab it into my eye if that would excuse me from sitting down and writing a budget," said Kent, a hard-working, highly paid, second-year associate, who had been lamenting that he never has enough money saved and can't get his credit cards paid off. His problem is not that he isn't earning enough, but that he doesn't know how to manage his money.

Many young professionals put off developing a budget until it's too late. Justifying the delay is easy to rationalize. For 20-somethings (especially single 20-somethings), the desire to enjoy the career that's just getting started is strong, including enjoying the fruits of hard work (e.g., cars, trips, clothing). When the 30s roll around, preoccupation with a mortgage and family responsibilities may begin. In the 40s, an unexpected health crisis, medical expense, or family emergency, as well as funding a child's college education, may become the focus. Unfortunately, by the 50s, it's often too late to adjust expenses and accumulate significant savings for a comfortable retirement. With age comes wisdom, but youth also has an advantage: the earlier you start saving, the better for your financial future. Consider this—even the Queen of England has need for a budget, as demonstrated by the January 2014 report from the Common Public Accounts Committee revealing that Queen Elizabeth II was down to her last $1.6 million. The report stated that the royal family was "spending above their means and dipping into the reserves . . . the balance now stands at an all-time low." Indeed, the Queen's reserve fund went from £35 million ($58 million) in 2001 to only £1 million ($1.6 million) in 2014. Spending without tailoring it to specific needs and goals can lead you to shortfalls, even if you start with millions.

The bottom line: whatever your age, don't fall into the common trap of mortgaging your financial future to indulge a lifestyle. Before you wander down the path of rationalization, take control of your finances now. Bringing expenses under control may be easier than you think.

PAGE THREE: THE BUDGET

Now, it's time to create the actual budget. Analyze pages one and two and ask, have I been living within my means? How much of my hard-earned money has gone to genuine needs and how many of the items could I have lived without? Distinguishing between what you "need" and what you "want" is critical to getting out of debt and building wealth. For example, people need food, shelter, and clothing. However, they may want perfume, cigarettes, football tickets, and new furniture. Many professionals find that they earn a decent income and are organized in their work life—and even their closets—but remain frustrated and vexed because they can't seem to save enough or pay off their credit cards. Finding a higher-paying job is often not the solution. This is because they must fundamentally change how they handle their money. Even if a fantasy of winning thousands of dollars came true, it wouldn't help, because when income isn't properly allocated, it is spent, triggering a hike in living standards. A new suit, a bottle of single malt scotch for the poker buddies, a newer car, replacing the hand-me-down furniture with sleek new designs—it doesn't take long for a young professional to accumulate an even higher stack of bills.

Start with the bare necessities for your budget, then add on in accordance with allocating for your short-term and long-term goals. Begin the budget with these general guidelines:

1. **Max Out Retirement Contributions.** This is especially important if your employer has a matching program. Determine what the maximum contribution is for the year, and divide by 12 for the monthly amount to be deducted from your paycheck.
2. **Six Months of Cash Reserves.** Build a safety net equal to six months' take-home pay to tackle any unexpected calamities such as loss of a job, medical expenses, or repair bills. The general rule is that the emergency fund should contain an amount equal to six months of your take-home pay. To estimate a monthly figure to include in your budget for emergency fund savings, try dividing six months of paychecks by 12. Then, factor that amount into your monthly plan. Put the money in a money market fund or a short-term certificate of deposit to maximize your interest earnings.
3. **Savings.** If you're maxing out on retirement contributions annually and have six months of cash reserves in place, consider whether to save more by investing, discussed in Chapter 7. The general rule is to save 10 percent of your take-home pay. For some, that 10 percent may be usurped by maxing out on retirement contributions. However, for many, there may be nothing left over after all other expenses have been paid. This is when you need to carefully scrutinize where you can cut back—even if only temporarily or periodically, such as redirecting the money you'd normally spend on weekend entertainment toward savings. Reducing the amounts you spend on discretionary or "want" items can further your savings goals. Also, arrange for your paycheck to be automatically deposited to your checking account. It's the easiest way to build net worth because you are less tempted to spend it.
4. **Living Expenses.** Allocate money for your rent or mortgage and property taxes, along with utilities.
5. **Food.** Allocate money for your daily food needs.
6. **Transportation.** Car payments, maintenance, gas, insurance, license and car registration, toll payments, and parking fees are legitimate expenses. For those without a car, include costs of public transportation.
7. **Health Care.** Premiums, co-pays, medication, dental fees, glasses, and contact lenses are all examples of unreimbursed expenses to budget for even if you have the best of employee benefit plans.

8. **Taxes.** If taxes (federal, state, Social Security) are not taken from your paycheck, factor them in with your budgeting. (Then, you'd start with gross salary as your income, not take-home pay).
9. **Children.** Although some expenses are necessary for child care, consider whether your child really needs another toy, a designer outfit, or private lessons. Child care, babysitters, medicine, and diapers are all expenses that are necessary, and you need to include them in the budget.
10. **Vacation.** Include vacations in your budget because sooner or later, everyone needs a break, and there's a much greater chance for relaxation instead of anxiety if you've financially planned for the trip. Set a little aside on a monthly basis. If you're broke, consider less expensive travel, such as hiking or a biking trip with friends. Even if it's just taking a long weekend, sleeping in, or staring at the wall while sipping martinis, remember to give yourself time to recharge.

Notice that savings-related concerns are the first items listed. Always pay yourself first—whether it's in the form of retirement contributions or a deposit to build the emergency fund—before you spend money on nonessential expenses. If you're in credit card debt, pay it off, but try to allocate money for your employer's matching retirement program, if any. Overall, it may not appear possible to pay yourself first, especially 10 percent of your monthly paycheck. Again, consider whether there are nonessentials that you are buying, and pay into savings what you can scrape together. If you can't handle missing the morning Starbuck's (or your coworkers can't handle your personality if you forgo the morning Starbuck's), implement a savings progression system. Anytime you get coins back from a cash purchase, deposit them in a jar. At the end of the month, deposit the money in the emergency fund savings account. You can also do this with larger bills. When you receive change from a $5 bill, deposit the dollar bills and change in the jar and at month's end in your emergency savings fund.

IMPLEMENTING YOUR BUDGET

If you're new to budgeting, sticking to it may be difficult at first. If you fall off the wagon once in a while, don't beat yourself up (because there are plenty of people you'll meet in your career who'll try to do that for you, but don't let them beat you up either). Examine why you went off track. Learn from it and move on. Conversely, if you're repeatedly outspending what you earn, find another system that works for you. Sticking to a budget can be like sticking to a diet. If you deprive yourself, you'll develop uncontrollable cravings for things and eventually fail to stick to the plan. This means don't put down $0 for Entertainment if you know you cannot live with it. A budget that doesn't leave money for an occasional, reasonably priced dinner out, or, when you have a family, an excursion together, will likely fail. Your budget is not meant to bind you to drudgery or a peasant's austerity.

Also, don't keep a lot of cash in your wallet. It's easier to splurge when cash is readily available to you. Direct deposit of paychecks and minimum cash withdrawals can help stop the hole in your safety net. Likewise, the most common slipups involve credit cards and record keeping. Remember, credit cards are not cash, especially when it comes to impulse spending. Regarding record keeping, it's important to keep track of the same expenses you listed when preparing your budget. Good records will help you keep track of where your money comes from and where it goes. Computer software programs can help track expenses and provide reports and graphs to illustrate what you're spending your money on. Recording purchases in a notebook, as well as keeping receipts for everything you buy, also works well. Another way to keep track is through your credit card statements, online banking records, or checking account statements. When you pay for purchases with checks or your credit card, you will have a monthly record of them. Also, remember to keep track of the items you purchase with cash. Whatever you do, use the system that works best for you.

At the end of each month, compare your actual expenses to your budget. Try to keep your spending within your plan, and look for ways to cut your expenses. Don't give up if maintaining your budget is hard for the first few months. It may take some time to set up a plan that works for you. Be flexible. If your budget is not working for you, fix it so it will. Computer software like Quicken can also help.

Finally, the budget need not be a well-honed document, but it should be thorough. Prevent napping at the financial helm by doing an annual checkup of your finances. Your budget will also require periodic updates or revisions to accommodate whatever event has occurred—a pay raise, family responsibilities, unexpected debt, or changes in the economy—that can affect your financial life. In summary, the budget is the cornerstone of effective financial planning. It begins with analyzing your current assets and liabilities, identifying your "wants" and "needs," and then developing a plan for you to live by month-to-month for paying current expenses while laying out a strategy for achieving your lifelong goals. It doesn't mean that you'll never be able to have your "wants"; it just means that for some of us, they have to be postponed. So, if you've been obsessing over the BMW or Porsche, stop tormenting yourself and give it a rest, at least until your debt is paid, your emergency fund is established, and your retirement contributions are maxed out. Now, take this vision you've sketched for your finances, and apply the budget to your life.

DEVELOPING A BUDGET FOR EFFECTIVE FINANCIAL PLANNING

1. Analyze current assets/liabilities and distinguish needs from wants
2. Research spending habits and actual expenses
3. Determine goals: being debt-free, saving for emergency protection, accumulating wealth, minimizing taxes, preserving wealth for retirement
4. Draft budget: meet present daily expenses and short-term, medium-term, and lifelong goals
5. Implement budget and periodic review, revise and update budget as necessary

Chapter 3

Student Loan Debt: The Good, the Bad, and the Ugly

Student loan debt collectors have power that would make a mobster envious.

—Professor Elizabeth Warren, Harvard Law School

Because student loan payments have a grace period on payment, they can seem like a sweet deal, but if you don't get a financial hold on them, they will leave a sour taste very quickly. If you graduated from a public law school, chances are you may be as much as $51,056 in debt ($78,763 or more if you graduated from a private law school), according to student loan debt statistics maintained by the ABA Section of Legal Education and Admissions to the Bar. Add in any college student loans and the median lawyer's starting salary of $60,000 will not be enough to pay your "ambitions tax"—the colloquial term coined for the financial price you have to pay for a graduate education these days. So, if you are a graduate whose student loan debt exceeds your starting salary—unless you have a benefactor to support you—you're going to have to learn to live with your student debt. Should you feel discouraged, inspiring stories of others who have paid off their loans—and tips that worked for them in doing it—can be found at http://www.smarterbucks.com/blog/how-i-crushed-my-90k-of-student-debt/.

To learn the amount you owe, start by consulting the National Student Loan Data System (http://www.nslds.ed.gov/nslds_SA/) for totals owed on federal loans. If you haven't yet graduated, contact your school's financial aid office before you leave school to learn options and what's best for you. Likewise, if you are unsure who your lender is, or how to contact your lender, your school's financial aid office is also helpful to consult. Ultimately, when it's time to begin making payments, your lender or servicer will establish a standard repayment schedule. (The model repayment plan establishes a minimum monthly payment amount of $50 with a maximum of ten years to repay the loan.) It may become important that you maintain contact with your lender over the life of your loan(s), especially if you experience a cash-crunch and difficulty in repayment. Similarly, if you have moved, provide your lender with current address information so that the company can provide you with the loan payment materials. The day after you graduate, withdraw, or drop to less than half-time status, the six-month grace period begins. Expect your first loan payment to be due 30–45 days after the end of the grace period. For debt-ridden young professionals, Consolidation, Loan Deferment, and Forbearance are the options for repayment. Each has unique advantages, disadvantages, and eligibility requirements, as we discuss next.

STUDENT LOAN CONSOLIDATION

Loan consolidation is for those with multiple loans, with different lenders, requiring borrowers to write more than one check for monthly payment. Loan consolidation enables you to bundle all your loans into a single loan with one lender and one repayment plan. With consolidation, the balances of your existing student loans are paid off, with the total balance rolling over into one consolidated loan. The result is that you have only one loan to pay. Both students and their parents can consolidate loans.

The benefits of loan consolidation are that it (1) locks in a fixed, possibly lower rate,[1] for the term of your loan; (2) lowers your monthly payment; and (3) combines everything into one monthly payment. In addition, consolidated loans should have no fees, charges, or prepayment penalties and may offer flexible repayment options. Obviously, you should consider consolidating your loans if the consolidation loan would have a lower interest rate than your current loans. Student loan providers such as Sallie Mae have proclaimed that consolidating student loans can reduce monthly payments by up to 54 percent. However, the only way to reduce your payment this much is to extend your repayment plan.

1. Although the interest rate for Stafford loans made after July 1, 2006, is fixed, loans prior to that date were made at a variable interest rate tracking the July 1 Treasury bills.

Typically, you have ten years to repay student loans. Depending on the amount you're consolidating, extending the repayment plan up to 30 years may be possible; however, the longer it takes to repay the loan, the more interest you're paying. It comes down to what amount you can manage to pay monthly while remaining true to your long-term financial goals. On the positive side, there are no prepayment penalties, so if you choose to extend the payments past ten years, you can always pay off the loan early. The negative is that for some borrowers, the only way to obtain the lowest interest rate is to extend the period of the repayment of the loan, which may result in more interest being paid. Also, if you are close to paying off your existing loans, consolidation may not offer you any savings.

The interest rate for the consolidated loan will be calculated by averaging the interest rate of all the loans being consolidated and then rounding up to the next one-eighth of 1 percent. You can calculate your interest rate by visiting www.salliemae.com or http://loanconsolidation.ed.gov/ and using the online calculator.

Whether loans qualify for consolidation depends on the following criteria: (1) you are in your six-month grace period following graduation, or you have started repaying your loans; (2) you have eligible loans totaling over $7,500; (3) you have more than one lender; (4) you have not already consolidated your student loans, or since consolidation you have gone back to school and acquired new student loans. Most loans are eligible for consolidation. To begin the consolidation process, check with your lenders that hold your current loans. It may be possible to consolidate through any bank or credit union that participates in the Federal Family Education Loan Program, or directly from the U.S. Department of Education. Generally, the loan terms and conditions will be the same, regardless of where you consolidate. However, if all your loans are with one lender, you must consolidate with that lender.

Importantly, you can only consolidate once, unless you go back to school and take out more loans. This means that you should do some research and make certain that you have found the best deal possible. Although the interest rate may be the same from all lenders, you may find some lenders that are willing to provide future rate discounts for prompt payment as well as a discount for having monthly payments directly debited from your checking account. If you are married, it is permissible for a married couple to consolidate loans but not advisable. This is because both of you will always be responsible to repay the loan, even if you later separate or divorce. Also, should you need to defer payment on the loan, both of you will have to meet the deferment criteria.

Regarding the time frame for consolidation, although you can consolidate your loans any time during your six-month grace period or after you have started repaying your loans, you have a better chance of getting the lowest rate if you consolidate during your grace period. Practically speaking, because you will lose the rest of the grace period, it is recommended that consolidation occur near the fifth month of the grace period. The consolidation process usually takes 30–45 days. With respect to private loans (non-government guaranteed loans), the interest rates and fees are usually higher than those for government-backed loans such as federal Stafford loans. Thus, consolidation should lock in a lower interest rate and save money for those graduates carrying private student debt. Graduates who consolidate during the grace period—the six months before you are required to begin monthly payments—could lock in a low rate, such as around 4 percent.

Consolidation is not available if you are still in school. A disadvantage to consolidation is that you may waive certain defenses. So, if you anticipate challenging the loan in court, certain arguments may be barred. Also, some financial experts may advise that the older your loan, the better your chance to negotiate a settlement with the lender on payment for a reduced amount, so it would be best not to consolidate old loans. Practically, this doesn't work for most graduates because to settle for a significantly reduced amount that would save you more money than consolidation, lenders usually require a lump sum cash payment of a major portion of the loan, and most graduates cannot afford the lump sum payment.

Finally, the decision to consolidate should not be automatic. If a lower interest rate is your goal, some lenders offer a discount for on-time payments (48 consecutive on-time loan payments) of up to two percentage points. Research what makes financial sense for you before you act. The calculators, mentioned previously, can run computations.

> Margaret, a new mother, began her career with a starting salary of $145,000 and with $200,000 in college and graduate student debt. The interest rate on $56,000 in private debt was 9.2 percent, for which she obtained a one-year forbearance on payment. She consolidated the remaining government-backed debt for a manageable 4 percent rate.

STUDENT LOAN DEFERMENT

A student loan deferment allows you some flexibility in repaying your student loans as long as you meet certain criteria. The primary benefit of deferment is that the payment and accrual of interest are suspended. Lenders typically extend a deferment for up to three years. To grant a deferment based on your economic situation, most lenders require you to apply every year and prove why you deserve to have your repayment suspended. Eligibility requirements may vary by lender, but the following are the most common:

Pregnancy or Adoption and Caring for a Newborn: If you are not working, are no longer in school, and have attended school at least half-time within the last six months, you may qualify for this student loan deferment. Proof, such as a doctor's statement/records, a copy of the birth certificate, or a statement from the adoption agency referencing placement, will be required. Certification from your school concerning your enrollment status may also be required. The deferment has a maximum time limit of six months. If you are unable to start repaying your student loans when the deferment expires, you may seek another type of loan deferment.

Economic Hardship: To qualify for this type of deferment, you need to have income below the "standard of living" as determined by the U.S. Bureau of Statistics. Keep in mind you may need to provide proof in this situation. For many, obtaining deferment because of economic hardship is difficult because you must be able to affirm that your monthly income does not exceed the larger of the federal minimum wage rate or the poverty line for a family of two (regardless of your actual family size). The lender will have worksheets to help you determine whether you satisfy this criterion.

Active Duty: Borrowers in the U.S. military, the National Oceanic and Atmospheric Administration (NOAA), or the U.S. National Guard in time of war or a state of emergency or officers in the Commissioned Corps of the U.S. Public Health Service may qualify for deferment.

Disability: In the unfortunate case that you may become disabled and unable to work for more than 60 days, or if you need to care for a disabled spouse or dependent for more than 90 days, then you may be eligible for deferment. To the extent you are totally and permanently disabled, U.S. federal student loans can be discharged, but not private student loans, absent a bankruptcy filing, which still requires a threshold showing of hardship, as discussed earlier.

Unemployment: You'll need to be working fewer than 30 hours per week or in a job that is not expected to last more than 90 days. You will likely also be asked to substantiate this, so it's wise to keep records about your job search efforts and documentation from any unemployment benefits. In most cases, an unemployment verification will be done to confirm your status.

Parental Status: Borrowers who have preschool-age children and are entering or reentering the workforce may qualify for a deferment. Federal PLUS loans are not eligible. The maximum cumulative time frame allowed for the deferment is 12 months.

Submit a deferment request directly to your lender. Most lenders offer forms online, so you can apply for a deferment by downloading the appropriate form, completing and signing it, and then sending it to the loan holder. Importantly, unless you receive notice that your deferment request has been approved, the loan payment due dates remain in place. Check with your lender or the company that services the loan for more information about processing. In general, deferments cost lenders money because they are not accruing interest on the debt. Thus, though a lender may initially be reluctant to discuss this option, a debt-ridden graduate should still inquire.

> John's starting salary was $75,000, and he had $92,000 in student debt. Because he had to relocate due to a hurricane, he negotiated a one-year forbearance. He then consolidated his loans to a more manageable 4 percent interest rate.

LOAN FORBEARANCE

Student loan forbearance is a worthwhile option to consider when you find yourself ineligible for student loan deferment. Student loan forbearance is granted at the discretion of the lender. Lenders usually grant forbearance if you are in poor health or experiencing other personal problems. Lenders must grant forbearance when your Title IV student loan debt equals or exceeds 20 percent of your gross income and you submit a written request. Under those circumstances, a lender must grant forbearance for one year and can renew it for a second and third year under certain conditions. Moreover, the fact that you are granted a forbearance cannot be the cause of a negative credit report and no fees can be charged. Unfortunately, this right is limited to loans held by lenders. It does not apply if the loan has been taken over by a guaranty agency or the Department of Education.

Generally, approval of a loan forbearance request is easier to get than approval of a payment deferment request. However, the downside of forbearance is that the interest continues to accrue, even though the loan payments are reduced or postponed. The benefit is that forbearance could allow you to avoid default (discussed later in this chapter) during the time you are unable to make payments. Once granted, a forbearance allows for a temporary postponement of student loan payments and an extension of the repayment schedule and may also allow for reduced loan payments. Though there are four types of forbearance, the two types that you can request from a lender are discretionary forbearance and mandatory forbearance, summarized next. (The other two types, administrative and mandatory administrative, are mainly used by the lender to apply to certain situations.)

You may be granted discretionary student loan forbearance when you can demonstrate that a certain financial hardship situation exists, impacting the repayment of your debt. Common situations that may qualify are: (a) being in school with an enrollment status of less than half-time (remember, if your status is more than half-time you may qualify for student loan deferment); (b) being unemployed (in the case when you have surpassed the maximum deferment time limit); (c) having poor health; (d) working fewer hours because of a reduction by your employer; or (e) experiencing a sudden change in life circumstance that impacts your income (for example, the community in which you live is designated a disaster area). Discretionary forbearance can also take the form of reduced payments. The benefit of reducing the monthly payment amount is that it may be more manageable for you.

Mandatory forbearance has specialized categories of eligibility (for which most people will not qualify): (a) you are participating in an internship/residency program (beyond the time frame requirements for a deferment); (b) you are in a national service position for which the National and Community Service Trust Act of 1993 applies; (c) you fall under the Teacher Loan Forgiveness Program; (d) you are participating in a qualifying service as defined by the Child Care Provider Loan Forgiveness Program; or (e) you are participating in qualifying service for partial loan repayment under the Student Loan Repayment Programs administered by the U.S. Department of Defense.

Interest is the primary difference between forbearance and deferment. You will always be responsible for all interest that accrues during the period of forbearance. During a deferment, you will be responsible for the interest that accrues if your loans are Unsubsidized Stafford Loans. If you have Subsidized Stafford Loans, you will not be responsible for the interest that accrues during a deferment. You can pay the interest during a period of forbearance or deferment—definitely the cheaper route in the long run; otherwise, your lender may capitalize the interest at the end of the forbearance/deferment period. When interest is capitalized, it will increase the amount of interest you have to pay.

A final point to consider is that forbearance may not automatically lock in the lowest interest rates. If you are carrying private student debt and locking in a lower interest rate is your primary concern, student loan consolidation should be pursued first or in conjunction with forbearance.

ALTERNATIVE REPAYMENT PLANS

Other than the standard loan payment schedule of paying the minimum payment set by your lender over ten years or less, your lender may offer other types of repayment schedules. Some plans may result in more interest being paid over the life of the loan, however. These plans are summarized in the following chart.

Federal Loan Repayment Comparison

Pay as You Earn	Income-Based	Standard
Only government-backed loans issued on or after October 1, 2007, are eligible.	Government-backed loans eligible without time restriction as to issuance.	Government-backed loans eligible without time restriction as to issuance.
10% of discretionary income payment cap	15% of discretionary income payment cap	$50 minimum fixed monthly payment
20-year repayment period	25-year repayment period	10-year repayment period

Graduated Repayment: Under this plan, monthly payments will gradually increase during your repayment period. The early payments are lower, which is both a positive and a negative. It is negative because it includes mostly interest, so you don't pay the balance quickly and you pay more interest. On the positive side, the manageability of the monthly payment is appealing because it anticipates that as you advance in your career, you'll earn more money to make the larger payment.

Income-Sensitive or Income-Contingent Repayment: Monthly payments will be based on the amount of money you earn. Between 4 and 25 percent of your gross income each month is paid over a 15-year period, or a 25-year period on the contingent plan. Some loans are not eligible.

Pay as You Earn: This option is available only to borrowers of federal direct loans who, prior to October 1, 2007, had never received a federal student loan and who received a loan disbursement after October 1, 2011. The amount of the monthly payment is 10 percent of the amount of your adjusted gross income that exceeds 150 percent of poverty level. You can estimate your payments with the calculator at https://studentloans.gov/myDirectLoan/mobile/repayment/repaymentEstimator.action.

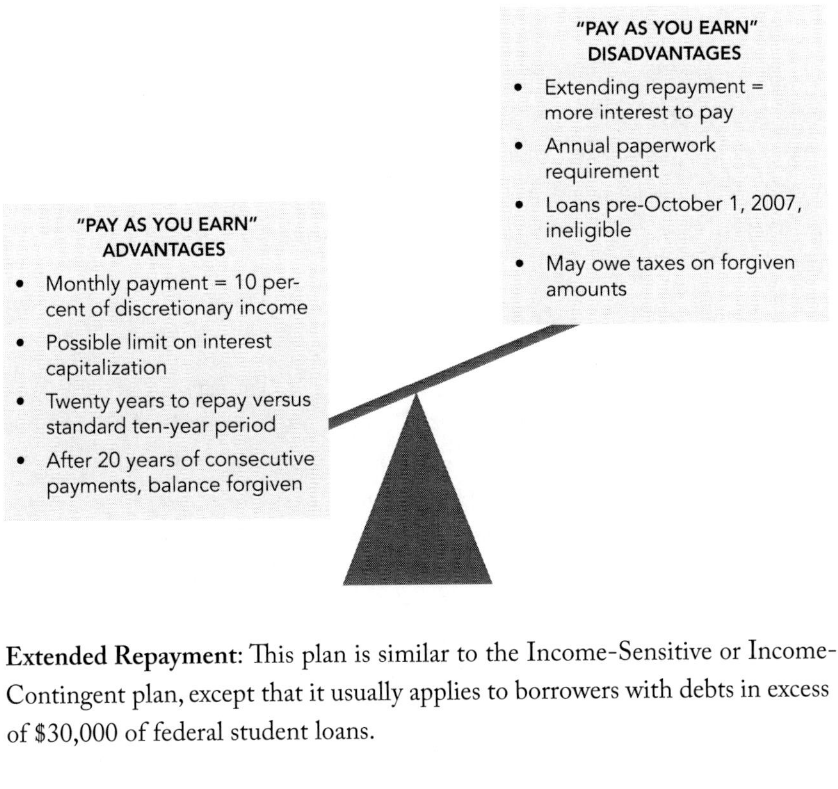

Extended Repayment: This plan is similar to the Income-Sensitive or Income-Contingent plan, except that it usually applies to borrowers with debts in excess of $30,000 of federal student loans.

Finally, you always have the option of prepayment, at any time, on all or a portion of the balance owed on your loan without penalty. Do-it-yourself calculators on forbearance, deferment, pay as you earn, consolidation, and the Public Service Loan Forgiveness Program (PSLFP) can be found at http://studentaid.ed.gov, http://paybacksmarter.com, or IBRInfo.org. A combination of approaches may best satisfy your needs. This is why contacting your lender to research and review your options is necessary before acting.

> Alisha, a legal aid lawyer, placed her loans in forbearance twice since graduating in 2001. Because of the accrual of interest, the loan balance increased from $21,000 to $28,000. After consolidating her loans, her monthly payment is now $175 versus $325, allowing room in her budget to fully participate in her employer's matching retirement plan.

LOAN REPAYMENT ASSISTANCE PROGRAM

Lawyers in public interest law may find that their state offers a loan repayment assistance program by way of grants or loan forgiveness. Eligibility for these programs varies greatly. Also, graduates should inquire of their alma maters whether the law school offers a loan payment assistance program. Often, law schools have easier eligibility requirements than those of state governments.

LOAN FORGIVENESS PROGRAM

The government limits the loan forgiveness program to certain child care providers and teaching, nursing, and military positions. Thus, most graduates do not qualify for this program. To the extent your lender offers debt forgiveness, be aware that loan forgiveness may bring tax consequences. Also, remember that the IRS considers forgiven or canceled debt as income, so a Form 1099-C "cancellation of debt" notice may follow debt collection. Creditors are required to file a Form 1099 with the IRS on forgiven debts of $600 or more. Yet, for most, after calculating the tax consequences, it may be that paying taxes on canceled debt is favorable to paying the debt off with after-tax earned income.

LATE PAYMENTS

Late student loan payments are reported to the credit reporting bureaus. This information may stay on your credit history for up to ten years—unless you rehabilitate the loan—and be considered by other lenders when you purchase a car or home and seek credit for other things.

LOAN DEFAULT

Despite the accumulation of interest, loan forbearance is a better alternative to default. For federally guaranteed student loans under Title IV of the Higher Education Act, default occurs when you fail to make payments on your loan for (a) 180 days if you repay in monthly installments or (b) 240 days if the payments are due less frequently. The lender must exercise "due diligence" during the time that you are behind in your payments. "Due diligence" involves the lender making repeated efforts to find you and contact you about repayment. Ultimately, the lender will turn the loan over for collection to the U.S. Department of Education or the guaranty agency in your state. Lenders may accelerate a defaulted loan, which means that the entire balance becomes due in a single payment. Also, the collection fees can be added to the loan for payment. A default will be reported to credit bureaus, and your credit rating may suffer because the default will show up in the negative on a credit report. Worse, the government is permitted to seize a borrower's tax refunds, garnish wages, and withhold other federal benefits, such as Social Security, if a loan is in default. Once a loan has been declared in default, it is no longer entitled to a deferment or eligible for forbearance. Likewise, you can be denied any further student aid should you pursue additional studies. Consequently, before allowing the loan to default, contact your lender to try to work something out. Most lenders would rather have a loan voluntarily paid than turn it over to collection. The key is not waiting until the last minute. Take affirmative steps to contact your lender and discuss the options that are available to you should you find yourself in a financially strapped situation.

LOAN REHABILITATION PROGRAM

Sometimes a defaulted loan may be reinstated by the Department of Education under its loan rehabilitation program. Typically, this requires 12 consecutive monthly payments, though you can also pay off your entire student debt in one lump sum. When you enter into a repayment agreement with your lender, guaranty agency, or collection agent, a new loan is created that wipes out the defaulted loan. The benefit of loan rehabilitation is that once a loan has been rehabilitated, it will be taken out of default, and the credit bureau reports made by the servicing agency will be deleted. Also, you will be able to repay the loan usually over nine years and regain eligibility for additional Title IV student financial aid funding should you pursue further studies.

BANKRUPTCY

If your obligation to repay a student loan is discharged in bankruptcy, any cosigners or endorsers of your debt are not discharged. For example, if your parents cosigned your student loan, they are still liable for repayment. Before you think bankruptcy is your best option, however, borrowers have an incredibly high burden of proof. To discharge student loan debt in bankruptcy, borrowers must essentially prove that they will fail to maintain a minimal standard of living if they are forced to repay and that such failure will continue into the foreseeable future. For a lawyer, filing personal bankruptcy is the equivalent of career suicide. To achieve discharge of the student loans, you're basically going to have to argue that you're never going to have a sustainable career.

In the 1970s, young professionals' filing for bankruptcy to rid themselves of student loan debt was commonplace. Congressional amendments to the Bankruptcy Code, however, have made the task more difficult. Courts will likely take into account practical considerations, such as whether the borrower can find a higher paying job or has done everything possible to try to cut the payments to a manageable amount and what types of efforts were made, if any, to attempt repayment before deciding to file bankruptcy. Any grace periods, forbearances, or deferments must be subtracted from the time elapsed between the date the first payment became due and the bankruptcy filing date, which can also be critical in calculating whether the debt will be discharged. In any event, before choosing bankruptcy as an option, it is strongly recommended that you investigate the other options detailed earlier in this chapter and discuss those options with your lender.

ERRORS WITH STUDENT LOANS

Errors in record keeping, such as payments not being credited properly, incorrect interest rates being assigned, and incorrect personal information being recorded, commonly occur. When you discover an error in your student loan, contact your lender immediately. If you are unable to resolve the error, contact the Federal Student Aid Ombudsman of the Department of Education at 1-877-557-2575. You may be able to manage your student loans online at https://www.salliemae.com/, which allows you to view the status of your loan, make payments, correct or update contact information, and, in some instances, change your payment plan.

TAX DEDUCTIONS

Subject to your satisfying certain criteria, the interest you pay on your student loans may be deductible. Eligibility depends on your income level and on whether the proceeds of your loan(s) were used to fund qualified higher education expenses (i.e., tuition, fees, room and board, school supplies). If you paid more than $600 in interest on your student debt during the year, the lender should send you a Form 1098-E, showing the amount paid. In order to claim this amount on your income taxes, a Form 1040 or 1040A must be filed. Unlike with mortgage interest, you do not have to itemize deductions to take advantage of this deduction.

STRATEGY FOR MANAGING STUDENT DEBT

Balance your immediate need for a low monthly payment with your long-term financial goals. Although lenders work within the confines of the promissory note, they would rather find a way to achieve voluntary payment of the loan to make it work for you. The goals for student debt are to get the interest rate as low as possible within the shortest time frame to pay it off. If that doesn't give you a manageable monthly payment and there are no other ways to cut back on your living expenses, then go for a longer payment plan since there should be no early pay-off penalties if circumstances change and you are able to pay the debt off sooner than anticipated. It is wise to include your student loan debt in the periodic review of your finances to ensure that you have obtained the most favorable terms possible for your financial situation. The key point to remember in managing your student loan debt is that until you contact your lender about options that may be available to you, it is unlikely your situation will improve.

Chapter 4

Credit: How to Use It Wisely

Credit buying is much like being drunk. The buzz happens immediately and gives you a lift . . . the hangover comes the day after.

—Dr. Joyce Brothers

For corporate types who understand how to structure business deals using debt as a tool for profit, seeing debt as the enemy in one's personal life can be difficult. However, the overall principle is the same: shrewdly managing debt in your overall financial structure can save you money. If you're using only one, low interest credit card, vigilantly paying off the balance every month so you accrue no interest or finance charges, you need read only the credit report section of this chapter. In contrast, if you're carrying a monthly balance on one or multiple credit cards with varying interest rates or if you have been denied credit or had a credit card rejected, read on.

CREDIT CARDS

Credit card use can overthrow, if not collapse, a healthy financial structure. Worse than being a slave to your paycheck is being dependent on the available balance of your credit card. If you are like many graduates, you used a credit card to help bridge the gap in your finances during school. According to a survey conducted by student lender Nellie Mae, grads leave school with an average credit card balance of $2,169 and may hold up to four credit cards with interest rates varying from 13.7 to 18 percent. Starting today, going forward, credit cards as a means of borrowing should be your second to last resort—the pawn and cash advance shops that charge more than 24 percent being the last resort. Why? Because a key component to financial success is paying off your credit cards. Truly, the simplest way to earn extra money, tax-free and risk-free, is to pay off your credit cards. If you're not forced to pay 18 percent interest, it's akin to earning 18 percent. The minimum monthly payment for most credit cards is about 2 percent of the balance, including interest. When you don't pay off your credit card each month, you're actually paying an inflated price for your purchases, while increasing the credit card company's profits.

> The purchase of a $2,500 chair at an annual interest rate of 18 percent takes 28 minimum monthly payments to pay off the balance. That's $5,896 in interest for the credit card company, bringing the real cost of the chair to $8,396, not to mention the lost savings and interest that could have been earned for you on the $5,896. In contrast, if you were able to redirect that minimum payment for 30 years into a monthly $50 deposit to an 8 percent account, you'd earn over $62,000.

Translation: Pay Off the Credit Cards!! Calculate debt pay-offs at http://www.creditcards.com/calculators/payoff.php. The intelligent way to use credit cards is to do the following:

1. Pay off the balance every month. When you pay off the monthly balance within the grace period, credit cards become an interest-free convenience. Be extra careful about paying within the grace period. Pay electronically, if possible, or mail the payment well before the deadline to avoid late payment accruals because some credit card companies can take up to seven working days to process a payment.
2. Research and select a card (American Express, Discovery, MasterCard, Visa) that offers you the lowest interest rate, a low or no annual fee, and no or limited finance charges. Cash-back or travel award programs may offer higher interest rates, so research what you're actually getting in exchange for paying for the privilege. Earning frequent flier miles is not a good reason to choose one card over another unless everything else is equal.
3. Use only one personal credit card. (If your employer provides you with a business card, obviously, only use the business card for authorized business purposes.) This practice reduces the urge to splurge and limits the number

of calls you have to make should it become lost or stolen. (Federal law provides that the most you will owe for unauthorized charges is $50 per card if you are unable to report your card lost/stolen before a thief uses it).

4. Avoid cash advances because those convenient checks occasionally delivered in the mail with your statement are not checks. They are worse than using your credit card because there is no grace period. The minute you cash the so-called check, interest starts running. There may also be a transaction fee of up to 3 percent of the cash advance total.
5. Invest in a shredder and destroy all discarded receipts, credit card statements (not being saved for tax purposes, discussed in Chapter 8), and even credit card solicitations to prevent identity theft.
6. One way to minimize the risk of identity thieves making unauthorized credit card transactions is to write "photo id required" on the back of your credit card so that a retailer has to ask for it when a purchase is made.
7. Review billing statements every month to confirm the transactions made on your account were purchases or charges you authorized. (You have 60 days to notify the credit card company in writing, with the company having 30 days to respond and 90 days to resolve or correct the error. You're not required to pay the disputed amount and should not incur any finance charges on the disputed amount while the company is investigating the matter.)
8. Should your Social Security number be stolen, set up a fraud alert for your Social Security number. Experian offers this option at https://www.experian.com/fraud/center.html and automatically notifies the other two credit bureaus that it has been done. A fraud alert expires after three months, but you can renew it for another three months, if needed.

DIGGING OUT OF DEBT

Alright, so you're on board with paying off the credit cards, except how do you do it? When you're running on empty, paying off the credit cards is easier said than done. If you've reached the point where you accept the fact that you've accumulated too much credit card debt, follow these steps:

Step 1: Pledge that you'll change the way you use credit cards to avoid falling back into the same financial hole.

Step 2: Store all credit cards in a safe, secure location where they won't become lost or stolen and you won't be tempted to use them.

Step 3: Develop a plan to pay down the debt by considering the following suggestions as well as reviewing the cost-cutting measures outlined in Chapter 2 concerning budget preparation.

Suggestions for becoming debt-free include the following:

Stop Using Credit Cards. Stop using your credit cards, and especially avoid retail store and gas station cards. If you slip and sneak a credit card quickie, destroy the credit cards. If you don't trust yourself, destroy them now. Regarding retail cards, close the accounts once they are paid off. The closing of the accounts may affect your overall credit score, discussed later in this chapter. However, the advantages of closing them are that it eliminates overspending and reduces identity theft opportunities.

Cash In Your Savings. The highest rate of return on your savings account is likely to be lower than the interest payment due on your credit cards. If you have savings, consider cashing it in to pay off the credit cards. Optimally, leave at least three months' worth of no-frills living expenses in the account. Another option is to borrow against any life insurance policies. Should you pass away before the balance of the loan is paid, the margin plus the interest can be deducted from any settlement that is due to your beneficiary.

Take Out a Home Equity Loan. If you own your home, you could qualify for a home equity loan that can take you from 18 percent interest payments to around 7 percent. Essentially, you're using your home as another credit card. The advantage is that if you itemize your deductions, at tax time, a portion of the interest may be deductible. Once the home equity proceeds pay off your credit card(s), do not use the credit card(s) or incur more debt until you have paid off the home equity loan. The mechanics of home equity loans are discussed in more detail later in the book. For now, know that a home equity loan should be viewed only as a one-time bail-out method for your high-interest consumer debt. Do not use it to transform your home into an ATM.

Refinance. If you haven't damaged your credit rating yet, refinancing may allow you to collapse your debts and roll them into a new mortgage. When interest rates are lower than the current mortgage rate, this option may make sense for you. Refinancing is discussed further in Chapter 5.

Borrow from Retirement. Most 401(k) plans allow you to borrow up to 50 percent or $50,000, whichever is smaller. The temptation to do so usually arises when one is in dire financial circumstances and the emergency funds have been depleted, the theory being that the 401(k) loan interest rate will be cheaper than the interest paid on the credit card(s). For most people, the downsides are the reasons to avoid borrowing from the 401(k). The downsides are (1) you will be paying back the loan with after-tax money, and the interest will be taxed again when you finally cash out the account at retirement; and (2) it will detour your savings progress. Importantly, if you quit or lose your job, the debt becomes due immediately. If you should be unable to pay it, the amount outstanding will be treated as a distribution. This means you'll receive a tax bill, including a penalty if you're under age 59½. Obviously, the best way to avoid the tax bill is to ensure the loan is paid off before you change jobs.

If you're one of the workers the Employee Benefit Research Institute's 2012 study reported already have a loan against their 401(k), know that if you are unable to repay the loan within five years, that loan will be deemed an early distribution with a 10 percent penalty, plus payment of state and federal income taxes for those under age 59½. In the event of job loss, the loan will have to be repaid within 60 days, or you will risk penalties and fees. To minimize the risk of defaulting on repayment, sign up for an automatic deduction of the loan repayments from your paycheck. Also, contribute as much as you can afford to the 401(k) account without having to borrow to pay for your daily living expenses.

Research the Best Card and Transfer Balances. Lawyers love fine print in practice, but surprisingly few actually read it in their personal transactions. Read the fine print of your credit card contract(s). If you have more than one credit card, make certain the highest balance owed is on the card with the lowest interest rate. Research whether there are costs associated with transferring balances to the lowest interest rate card. A 1 percent transfer fee or $50 is common, and when you transfer several balances, that adds up, so calculate over time whether the fees are worth it in comparison to the amount of interest you would be paying. Be cautious of unsolicited credit offers. Mail solicitations often pronounce a fantastically low interest rate effective during the promotional period. Before credit card hopping, inquire what the interest rate will be when the promotional period ends as well as the date the promotional period ends. Obviously, if you're switching cards, the new rate should not be higher than the one you're switching from. Also, some offers only apply the low interest rate if the balances have been kept for 12 months or if the balance is paid off within the promotional period. Finally, some introductory offers carry a penalty for transferring the debt to another card when the promotional period of low interest is over—another reason to ask questions and read the fine print. Transferring balances and closing accounts may negatively affect your credit scores, as discussed later in this chapter, but if you're swimming in debt, the first goal is to get rid of it. There are better ways to improve your credit than continuing to keep high-interest accounts open that you will be too tempted to use.

Renegotiate Terms with the Credit Card Companies. When you've exhausted all alternatives, including having nothing to sell or cash in, contact your creditors and renegotiate a new, lower repayment schedule. You might begin by researching the interest rates of other credit cards and inquiring whether your company can match the deal to keep you as a customer. Or you can simply explain that you can't afford to pay and learn what the company can do for you, if anything, to lower your repayment schedule. It should be mentioned that there are organizations specializing in guiding people out of debt. The "debt doctors" will contact your creditors and try to negotiate lower monthly payment requirements and interest rates. Be aware, however, that you also incur a monthly fee for these services. As an educated professional, consider taking the time to contact your credit card companies yourself, especially if this is the first time you've gotten into serious financial trouble.

Borrow from a Relative or Friend. If you're not proud, or if you are and can swallow your pride long enough to ask a relative or friend for a loan, consider this option. As all lawyers know, be sure to document the loan with a written agreement detailing a schedule for repayment and the interest rate. From an interpersonal perspective, if you choose this option, choose your source wisely, as there may be psychological ramifications to your relationship, unless you borrow from a pessimist, as Groucho Marx joked, because they never expect to be repaid.

Personal Bankruptcy Is the Last Resort. Besides the legal fees and the ten-year stain on your credit record, a personal bankruptcy filing will not likely help a lawyer's career. Proceed with this option using extreme caution and only as a last resort. Your second-to-last resort should be talking to your creditors to see if you can work something out. Some creditors may allow you an extra couple of months to catch up on debt, in exchange for tacking on missed payments at the end of the loan. Nevertheless, should your negotiations fail, there are two types of personal bankruptcy relief: Chapter 7, which allows the discharge of most debts except for alimony, child support, taxes, loans obtained through filing false financial statements, loans not listed in the bankruptcy petition, legal judgments against the petitioner, and student loans; and Chapter 13, which allows for a wage-earner plan by which you may keep most of your property under a court-approved repayment plan based on your resources that pays off all or part of your debt over three to five years. The benefits of a bankruptcy filing are that any creditor harassment must stop when you file, and, under Chapter 13 when all provisions of the court-approved plan are met, you emerge debt-free.

Avoid the Minimum. What do we think of people who only do the minimum? The line from the movie *Office Space* applies to credit cards: Never do the minimum. Though you may not be able to pay off the whole amount, scrape together every penny that you can and pay as much as you can above the minimum. The more you pay down every month, the faster that debt disappears, sometimes years sooner. Consider the following chart, which illustrates a $20 minimum payment on a $1,000 debt versus adding an extra $20 a month and paying $40.

	Interest Rate	Months to Pay	Total Payments
$20/month	6%	56	$1,126.97
	12%	67	$1,353.43
	18%	89	$1,783.97

For an Extra $20 . . .

	Interest Rate	Months to Pay	Total Payments
$40/month	6%	25	$1,025.24
	12%	27	$1,103.28
	18%	29	$1,199.00

Deter Solicitations. Contact one of the three U.S. credit bureaus and request removal from all prescreened credit offer lists. Those credit bureaus are Equifax, Experian, and Trans Union. Limiting solicitations also limits the risk of identity theft. Identity thieves commonly intercept solicitations, substitute their own name and address, and then max out the card before you know what's happening.

Exercise Patience. Impatience often leads to borrowing money to buy things that quickly depreciate and lose value, such as cars, clothing, and furniture. Consequently, you pay much more for the item than the price tag shows when the interest on the credit card or other loan is added. If you can't afford it, don't charge it. Wait, save, and then buy when you can pay cash or can pay off the charge (and total balance) when the item appears on your credit card statement.

Once the credit cards are paid off, before you use credit again, consider what kind of spender you are. Take the Spender Quiz in Appendix B, and you may learn more about your money attitudes and habits.

> If you don't think your credit card use is a problem, ask yourself whether you: (1) are living paycheck to paycheck and have little or no savings; (2) have more than two credit cards and pay only the minimum balance; (3) were denied credit or had your credit card rejected; (4) compulsively buy things you don't need or use when you shop; or (5) use cash advances to pay bills. A yes answer suggests that credit card use is likely at a financially dangerous level. Remember, there's no quick fix to carrying too much debt, except to stop the spending habits that brought the debt about in the first place.

FINANCING A CAR

Don't. If you can afford to pay cash, do it. The exception to the rule is 0 percent financing when it's coupled with a reasonable sales price. In fact, when dealers advertise interest rates on sale, a good shot at getting a good price is to inform the dealer you'll be paying cash.

However, because not everyone can afford to pay cash for a BMW or Porsche and 0 percent isn't usually available, young professionals should consider purchasing a less expensive new car or gently pre-owned (used) car. The overall savings isn't just in the purchase price but also insurance, maintenance, operating costs, and financing. If the savings on purchasing a compact or pre-owned car equaled a $10,000 bonus in your pocket, would you still care about whether your colleagues will be impressed by your parking something more fancy in the office garage? (The financially healthy answer to that question, assuming you don't have your credit cards and student loans paid off and an emergency savings fund established and are financially unable to max out your annual retirement contribution, is no.)

Nevertheless, if your transportation needs dictate that you finance a car, borrow as little as possible at the lowest rate you can find for the shortest period of time.

Concerning a dealer's promotional rates, be wary. An attractive interest rate can be used to distract you from an unattractive price. (Most car dealers, when interrogated, will eventually admit that you can get a better price if you pay cash rather than the dealer incentive rate.) Remember that banks and credit unions also offer attractive interest rates, sometimes better than dealers. Avoid buying a dealer's extended warranties or accident insurance; the dealer's price is not worth the benefits. Similarly, credit life insurance—which pays off the loan balance if you die—is only a good deal if you are unfortunately terminally ill, but then there is a preexisting condition clause that may apply to bar recovery.

Unless you have your own business and intend to use the car for business travel, do not lease. Although leasing a car requires the least cash down, you are paying the most to finance the car over the long run with no equity (or paid-up used car) to show for it in the end.

HOME EQUITY LOAN

A home equity loan involves a line of credit secured by your home that you may draw upon and pay back, in full or in part, as often as you like. This financing method can be just as advantageous as it can be dangerous. If you are someone who has difficulty controlling your credit card spending, don't refinance your home. Think about it—it's like having a huge credit card with a longer time to repay. If there's nothing forcing you to pay off that new car you purchased with your equity line of credit, you probably won't and will be tempted to sink deeper into debt instead. Also, because the line of credit is tied to the general level of interest rates, when rates go up, so will your payment. If you can't pay, there goes your home in foreclosure. Home equity loans are designed for the self-disciplined borrower. The best terms are those with no points (service fees a lender will charge up front to make the loan and to make a profit) and minimal up-front fees.

> Ruben and his wife paid off their student loans, credit cards, and car loans with a home equity loan. The resulting new, larger home equity mortgage payment required two incomes. Unfortunately, they divorced. Neither could afford to keep the home, and they had no equity, so when the home sold, they had nothing to show for it.

CREDIT SCORES: INFORMATION THAT GOES INTO THEM AND HOW TO IMPROVE THEM

As you probably know, lenders and others will look to your credit score to determine whether to extend you a loan or credit card and set the interest rate. A credit score can also affect whether a landlord will rent you an apartment, and even the amount of a deposit you have to pay for utilities. The score is based on various information that is reported to three credit bureaus (Equifax, Experian, and TransUnion) by past and current creditors about your financial history, as well as by independent companies. Though VantageScore is in use by some lenders, the most commonly used method to determine your score is the FICO score. FICO scores range from 300 to 850. The higher the score, the easier it will be for you to obtain credit at a low interest rate. Most lenders classify FICO credit scores above 700 as very good and an indication of good financial health. If it is below 620, on the other hand, lenders usually place a borrower in the "subprime" category. This category translates to higher interest rates, and applications can even be turned down. Of the three credit bureaus that maintain credit information about you, each determines its own score for you. Lenders and others purchase credit reports about you from these bureaus for purposes of determining, among other things, whether to extend credit, rent to you, or adjust your credit card interest rate. If information changes at the bureau about your financial history, then your credit report changes—which means you always have the opportunity to improve your score.

Because a FICO score covers various types of information, no one factor, listed above, will determine your score. Similarly, as the information in your credit report changes, so does the importance of the preceding factors in determining your score.

Lenders also look at several other things when making a credit decision—income, length of time at your present job, and the type of credit for which you

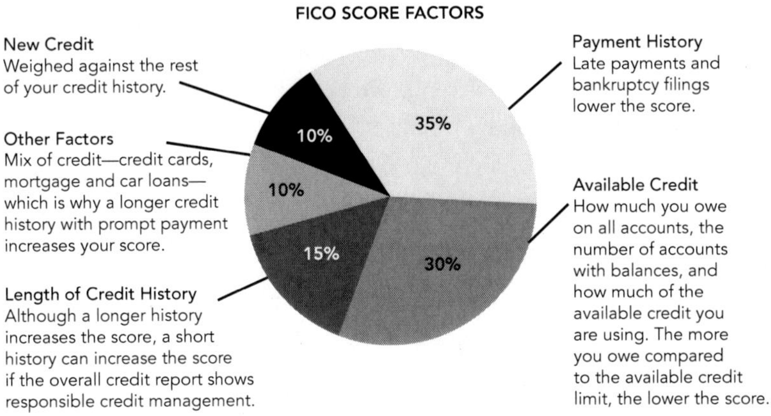

are applying. Nevertheless, improving your credit score can improve the picture lenders see of your creditworthiness and, thus, qualify you for lower interest rates. There are six ways to improve your credit score: (1) pay bills on time; (2) because high debt levels hurt your score, pay off monthly balances, or at least get the balances low on credit cards and avoid revolving balances; (3) pay down the cards that are maxed out first because points are deducted any time you charge more than 50 percent of the limit; (4) get current and stay current on debts because the longer your history shows payment of bills on time, the better the score; (5) only apply for or open new accounts if you really need them (the number of inquiries made for new account/loan applications results in a lower score because when consumers anticipate money problems they try to increase their credit lines); and (6) review your credit report annually for accuracy and contact the credit reporting bureau from which you obtained the report and the creditor to correct any errors or omissions you find. Verify that "closed by consumer" appears for all accounts you've closed. Checking on your own credit report does not negatively affect your score; only the inquiries and frequencies of others pulling your credit report are factored.

Importantly, sometimes the very things that can advance a healthy financial future—such as not using credit cards and paying a debt off—can negatively affect your credit score. Lenders will tell you that not using credit cards, closing accounts, and transferring debt to the credit card with the lowest interest rate make it difficult for the credit-scoring formula to generate a score for you. However, you don't have to owe balances and pay interest to have a good score, you just have to use credit once in a while; for example, make a purchase when you know you'll be able to pay off the charged item during the grace period so no interest accrues. The negative effect of closing an account will be minor if you have a high credit score. It will be major if you have a troubled financial history, but if you close out your accounts slowly over several months and close out your newest accounts first so that you don't lose the longer credit history, you can reduce the negative effect on your score. When comparing the potential negative effect of closing an account to becoming debt-free, consider that if your credit history is troubled or you've maxed out your credit limit, that's all the more reason to work on paying off the debt rather than trying to acquire more credit and generate even more debt until bankruptcy is inevitable. After all, your credit scores can change when new information is reported by your creditors. Plus, both positive and negative information goes into your credit report. So, if you have late payments on your report, but you establish and reestablish a good record of making payments on time, that will raise your score. This means that for a debt-ridden graduate, the score will inevitably improve over time so long as credit is managed responsibly.

You have the right to see what the bureaus are reporting about you when they provide a lender with a credit report. Under the Fair and Accurate Credit Transactions Act, Equifax, Experian, and TransUnion are required to provide consumers with a free credit report, once a year, upon the consumer's request. Though scores are built on changing information (e.g., pay off a credit balance and your score increases, apply for a new account and your score decreases), most FICO scores change around 20 points a quarter. When you conduct your annual review of your financial status, go ahead and order your credit report. An annual review will help to correct errors and alert you to unauthorized transactions in potential identity theft situations.

One way to learn more about your credit score is to look at "reason codes." According to ReasonCode.org, these codes are numerical explanations of a credit score. The reason codes may be called different names—adverse action code, score factor—but they provide descriptive information about why your credit score is that number.

Presuming that the information correlating to the reason codes is correct, learning the reason codes can help you improve your credit score by implementing changes to certain financial habits. Here is an example of how a credit report may list a score and the reason codes for it:

Credit Score: 680

- 32: Balances on revolving accounts are too high in comparison to limits.
- 16: Total balances on open accounts are too high.
- 12: The date that you opened the oldest is too recent.

Options to improve a credit score corresponding to the preceding example's reason codes would include paying down debt and aging or keeping the oldest credit account open to increase the overall credit history duration.

Should you receive a credit score report without explanations behind the reason codes, go to ReasonCode.org to find out what the numeric codes mean. ReasonCode.org is powered by VantageScore.

AVOID PIGGYBACKING

Piggybacking is a controversial method for potentially boosting your credit score. You are listed as an authorized user of a credit card belonging to someone whose credit history is healthy. You don't get to use the credit card, but the credit history of that card appears on your credit report, making your report more attractive. Internet sites offering these techniques pay the credit holders who are making their credit available. The consumer with the damaged score pays the Internet site a hefty fee, and some may even be offered a high-interest credit line for use.

The practice is controversial because some argue it violates Federal Trade Commission and banking laws as well as supports identity theft against those who are offering up their credit histories. Others counter that it's no different than getting someone to cosign a loan. If you decide to do it, don't believe everything you read on the company's website, especially with respect to money-back guarantees, and pull your credit report to ensure that information is being correctly reported. Before you sign up, however, consider that the money you will use to pay the site would likely be put to a better purpose paying down your debt.

It should be mentioned that even if you trust the person adding you to his or her card, some credit companies will refuse to report you—even as an authorized user—to the credit bureaus. The cardholder should inquire whether the credit history will be reported to the appropriate bureaus for you; if not, there's no point in risking the credit history of someone you trust—should you make purchases and default, which will then bring down your good Samaritan's credit score. Bottom line: borrowing another's record can be risky for everyone involved.

FICO SCORE 9

Starting with the Fall of 2014, FICO announced for customers with paid collections on their accounts a new scoring program called FICO Score 9. Essentially, it ignores paid collection accounts. VantageScore 3 from VantageScore also ignores repaid collection actions, though as noted previously, VantageScore is not as commonly used as FICO. The FICO Score 9 program provides less weight to paid medical collection debts than other types of collection accounts. So, if you have a problem with timely payment of a particular hospital or doctor bill because of an insurance matter, for example, the FICO Score 9 option—if used by your lender—may keep the credit report history in good standing. All lenders have their own costs and internal requirements for transitioning to the use of FICO Score 9, however. Specifically, the testing also referred to as "validation" can involve a lender performing analysis of whether the FICO Score 9 program fits its respective needs before a lender decides to adopt the FICO Score 9 program. Running 'what if' scenarios implementing FICO Score 9 in comparison to a lender's current credit risk analysis program, for the purpose of determining whether it still filters through the risky credit applicants, is a time-consuming endeavor. Costs for implementing the option may also be a factor as to whether a lender decided to adopt the FICO Score 9.

Chapter 5

Housing: It's Not How Much Mortgage You Qualify for, but How Much You Can Comfortably Afford to Pay

To be an American is to aspire to a room of one's own.
—*New York Times,* "Dream House," April 19, 1987

Let your budget be your guide in considering when to buy a home and how much home to buy. Ideally, you should have enough money saved for a 20 percent down payment (that's in addition to the emergency fund and maxing out your annual retirement contribution), though lenders and realtors may tell you that a 5 to 10 percent down payment is sufficient if you have good credit and a job. However, just as home quality is not measured by square footage, neither is the quality of your life. There's no shame in renting a 500-square-foot studio if you're happy there. Quite simply, if you're not emotionally or financially ready to buy a home yet, don't do it just because society dictates that's what people do when they're your age.

REASONS TO RENT

The common argument for owning over renting is that rent is money down the drain versus a mortgage that builds equity and offers a tax deduction. Owning a home can also be a good inflation hedge. However, there are four arguments in support of renting: (1) your city's housing prices tend to be obscenely inflated (e.g., New York City, Los Angeles, San Francisco); (2) you'll be moving in fewer than five years because it takes at least five years to recoup the money you pay in up-front and selling costs; (3) you don't have the time, money, or energy to personally handle upkeep/maintenance of a home or hire it out; and (4) a devastatingly low FICO score results in an onerously high interest rate (i.e., hundreds of dollars more in your mortgage payment), and you have no money to pay a large down payment or you do not have significant cash reserves saved.

With respect to the tax benefits, the question is whether the mortgage deduction cuts your taxes enough to make owning a place cheaper than renting one. Figure the tax savings and determine whether it costs more to own than rent. If so, then the question to answer is whether the extra expense of owning a home brings you (1) greater enjoyment and (2) the potential for the value of the property to appreciate.

BUYING A HOME

When it comes to financial transactions, what matters most isn't the price, but what you're left paying, or receiving, after tax. As discussed more in Chapters 7 and 9, taxes cut the true return on most investments. Moreover, tax savings can cut the true cost of the deductible expenses, presuming you have enough deductions to itemize. So, though real estate agents and loan officers may ply you with computations of how much mortgage you can qualify for to purchase the McMansion on the hill, consider these three questions: (1) how much of the purchase price should you borrow; (2) should you go for a 15-year or 30-year loan; and (3) should you take a fixed- or adjustable-rate mortgage (ARM)? These questions will help you determine what amount you can afford to comfortably pay for your home—meaning, you'll not be so financially strapped that you're unable to sleep at night, and you won't have to live life like a peasant in a cavernous, 7,000-square-foot hut.

DEBT-TO-INCOME RATIO FOR A CONVENTIONAL MORTGAGE[1]

As a general rule, a monthly mortgage payment (including principal, interest, real estate taxes, and homeowners insurance) should not exceed 28 percent of gross monthly income.

Gross Income	Housing Expense Max 28% Monthly	Debt-to-Income Max 36% Monthly
$50,000	$1,167	$1,500
$60,000	$1,400	$1,800
$70,000	$1,633	$2,100
$80,000	$1,867	$2,400
$90,000	$2,100	$2,700
$100,000	$2,333	$3,000
$125,000	$2,916	$3,750
$160,000	$3,733	$4,800

So, before you go home shopping, calculate how much housing expense you can manage by multiplying your annual salary by 0.28, then dividing by 12 (months). Next, calculate your total monthly "debt obligation" by multiplying your annual salary by 0.36, then dividing by 12 (months). The result is your maximum allowable debt-to-income ratio. The debt obligation includes student loans, credit cards, car loan, child support/alimony, and the mortgage.

THREE APPROACHES TO HOME BUYING

Lenders offer different types of mortgage products. Although no single loan is best for all situations, there are three approaches to keep in mind when selecting what kind of mortgage is right for your overall financial strategy.

1. FHA and VA government-backed loans have different debt-to-income ratios.

(1) Borrow as Little as Possible for as Short a Time as Possible

When you're shopping for mortgage funds, consider this question: Why buy more of something than you need, especially if the product costs more than what you could earn if you saved the money? Borrowing for 15 years versus 30 usually adds little to your monthly mortgage payment. Think of a 15-year loan as a forced savings program: after 15 years, you'll have paid off the loan and have essentially saved the value of your home, increasing your net worth. If you are unable to qualify for a 15-year, take out the 30-year and pay extra to principal each month to accomplish the same goal. Make certain that there are no prepayment penalties associated with the 30-year, however.

Loan Term	Interest Rate	Loan Amount	Monthly Payment	Total Payments	Total Interest Paid
15 years	6%	$200,000	$1,633.11	$293,959	$93,539
30 years	5.77%	$200,000	$1,169.69	$421,086	$221,086
After 15 years, you've paid off, and in effect saved, $200,000. After 30 years, you'll only have paid off/saved $57,375.21. Scrape together an extra $250 per month to pay to principal for the 30-year, and it will be paid in 20 years, saving $86,267.23 in interest.					

Regarding whether to choose a fixed- or adjustable-rate mortgage, if the rates and fees for both types of mortgages are the same, go with the fixed because the risk of an adjustable rate soaring and creating an out-of-control monthly payment is eliminated.

Adjustable-rate mortgages (ARMs) are tied to one of two independent indices: U.S. Treasury securities or the cost that banks and savings and loans pay to borrow funds. A margin of 2 to 3 percent is added to the index rate, resulting in the mortgage rate for an "adjustment period." The adjustment period is the amount of time between rate adjustments. Only when interest rates are high and the adjustable rate is considerably cheaper, with a cap on how much the rate can rise in any one year and over the life of the loan, should an ARM be selected over the fixed rate. (In essence, refinancing achieves the same goal as taking out an adjustable-rate mortgage when rates are at an all-time high; that is, as the rates drop, you benefit from a better rate.) There's also the "convertible" adjustable rate, which provides an option of locking in a fixed rate after a specified number of years, when interest rates have fallen. But, the adjustable-rate mortgage is the cheapest, according to the broker or loan officer, right? Well, the adjustable-rate market can be deceptive. A low initial rate is usually a promotion. The important question is, what will the rate be after the first adjustment? Practically speaking, after the first adjustment occurs is when the loan is starting—not at the come-hither rate—and that's the number you should use when comparing alternatives. Also, make certain that the cap on the adjustable rate is not just on your monthly payments. There can be a back-ended situation in which any excess above the cap may be tacked on as additional principal; consequently, additional monthly payments are added to the back end of the loan (e.g., a 30-year loan becomes a 32-year), or the monthly payment stays high long after interest rates have dropped. As to fixed and adjustable rates, lenders are continually creating new products every week, but remember this pearl of wisdom that is common to all: If you cannot afford a higher fixed-rate loan, you cannot afford to buy the home. If, but for the low initial rate promoted by the adjustable-rate mortgage, you can't pay your monthly payments, walk away.

(2) Max Out the Amount Borrowed and the Term

Often, new homeowners will take out the maximum amount the lender says they qualify for at the longest term (30-year) so they can afford more house. Don't fall into this trap. This method only makes sense for the truly wealthy as a financial strategy, not as a strategy for those financially struggling to buy more house. If you lock in a bargain 30-year fixed rate, when rates zoom up, you're protected. When rates plunge, the loan is paid off and refinanced at a lower rate. The wealthy are the ones who can afford to do this because paying additional closing costs for the refinancing is chump-change for them, plus they're not forced to sell the home to pay for the next one if their work or lifestyle requires them to move. For those who have to make their paychecks stretch to accomplish their financial goals (and just pay the bills month-to-month), this method is less advantageous because it builds little equity should you have to sell in less than ten years, and it is more expensive in the long run with you paying interest to the lender instead of to your savings or advancing your investments. In fact, many fall into the trap of scrapping together the down payment and closing costs, then going even more into debt by using credit cards to deck out their new home and fund living expenses. If you choose this method, make sure you have enough of a financial cushion to max out the annual retirement contributions and save for other financial goals.

Though the urge to splurge on decor and new furnishings for your new home may be great, if you can't pay cash for it, don't buy it. Otherwise, the dream home will likely propel you into financial struggles for a very long time.

(3) Borrow Nothing at All

If you can afford to, when the cost of borrowing is high, it may be better to borrow nothing at all. After all, in negotiations, a cash offer can carve a few thousand off the purchase price. Average costs for a mortgage are $3,000 per $200,000 loan, plus the time of completing the application process. This method makes sense when your after-tax calculations show that the money you have sitting in investments is earning less than a mortgage would cost you. Built into this method is the carefree feeling of being debt-free, which for those with nervous stomachs is a plus. Of course, you'd still leave enough in your account for the emergency fund discussed in Chapter 1. It should also be mentioned that if you choose this method, don't waive the home inspection. Regardless of how much you love the home, a professional building inspector can identify (unseen) problems that are inherent in the property. (Watch the movie *The Money Pit* if you are in doubt about this worthwhile endeavor.)

OTHER CONSIDERATIONS BEFORE APPLYING FOR A MORTGAGE

Before you begin the mortgage application process, be aware of these practices:

Online Lending. Disclosing personal information online should always be carefully scrutinized. You may opt to call the lender and provide your information over the phone should you decide an online mortgage lender is for you. Regardless, the Internet is a good resource for researching rates and fees. Those who don't have a high FICO score are likely to find brokers to be the source of best rates for them. However, be careful because brokers will be charging a fee for matching you with a lender.

Annual Percentage Rate (APR). APR is the annual finance charge, which includes the costs for loan origination fees, mortgage insurance, and points. The points are a percentage of the loan that you pay up-front to "buy down" the interest rate on the mortgage. One point equals 1 percent of the loan and typically lowers the interest rate by 0.25 percent (e.g., one point on a $200,000 loan would be $2,000). Paying points makes sense if you won't be selling the home in less than five to ten years; otherwise, it's unlikely you'll have the time to recoup the costs. When comparing interest rates for fixed rates, you have to take into consideration the APR and points to understand what the true cost of the loan will be. A seemingly low interest rate doesn't necessarily mean it's the best deal for you without comparing the APR for rates and fees. Because the rate used for the ARM is likely to change, the APR cannot be used for comparison, however.

Credit Report. Most lenders follow the FICO score as the gauge for a borrower's creditworthiness. Though the number for qualifying for a mortgage varies among lenders, expect that if your credit score is below 620, you may be asked to increase the down payment and substantiate that you are worth the lending risk with bank statements and sources of income. Compare mortgage interest rates to FICO scores, and calculate your own score at http://www.myfico.com/myfico/creditcentral/loanrates.aspx. If you're about to apply for a loan, keep the credit card accounts open so that there's less likelihood that a closed account could decrease your score. (Keeping an account open for purposes of a loan application does not mean charging it up, sabotaging your debt-free goals.) For the reasons discussed in Chapter 4, it is imperative that your credit history be the best possible before you apply for a mortgage. This includes making certain that the report's information is accurate. A 2004 study found one out of four people had serious errors on their credit reports, so make certain you are not that unfortunate person before applying for a loan. Also, don't pad the region with loan applications because that will lead to multiple inquiries for your credit report. The frequency of inquiries can decrease the FICO score that a lender will consider in making the loan. Your own inquiries about your credit report will not count against you, so review your credit reports for any mistakes before applying for a loan.

Avoid Becoming House Poor. Typically, the maximum loan you'll qualify for is always greater than what you can comfortably afford to pay monthly. If the lender tells you that you qualify for a mortgage amount that is greater than your rent, yet you're barely managing to pay the rent, you obviously shouldn't commit to that mortgage payment. Likewise, it's easy to be persuaded by a realtor that you'll grow into a house, but that doesn't mean that your paycheck will, too. Plus, years of sacrificing dinners out, travel, and other pleasures to pay the mortgage can transform your dream house into a prison. Buying a home that is less expensive frees you to enjoy fun things without getting over your head in credit card debt. Paying extra to principal for an early pay-off of your mortgage is also an option. Keep this general rule as a backdrop when talking with lenders and realtors: the sales price should be less than two and a half times your income. For illustration purposes, this means that if your income is $60,000, then the home price should be $150,000 or less.

Job History. Be prepared if the lender asks you for a letter showing that you've satisfied the probationary period of your job if you've been there less than a year. Applicants with years at the same job are more likely to be approved than those who have been hopping from job to job. The exception is if you're switching jobs within the same occupation for a higher salary.

REFINANCING AN EXISTING MORTGAGE

But for the cost of paying points and closing costs, homeowners would refinance an existing fixed-rate mortgage every time the rates drop. The question becomes whether it's worth the closing costs and effort to refinance. If refinancing will knock 2 percent off your fixed interest rate, and the points and mortgage interest are fully deductible, maybe it's worth it to you. As with everything, do your research and analyze what is the best deal. For example, compare a 7 percent loan that charges no points to a 7.5 percent loan that charges 2.5 points. The first loan costs less initially, but after awhile, the savings at the basic rate of 7.5 percent may outweigh the points you paid up front if you hold the loan for a long period. So, if you expect to be holding the loan for a long time, take the 7.5 percent loan that charges 2.5 points; otherwise, the 7 percent would be the better option, especially if you intend to move in five to ten years. Just as with other mortgages, shop around, but ask your lender what's available first to see if it is willing to offer the best rate to keep your business.

> Forty percent of those age 55 and older surveyed in 2013 for Northwestern Mutual felt that paying off their mortgage was the best decision they ever made.

Chapter 6

When Your Iceberg Melts: Insuring for Catastrophes

If something can go wrong, it will.

—Murphy's Law

Just as Murphy's Law can occur at any time in trial practice, so it can in life. If you're thinking, "I can skip this chapter because I'm healthy," don't. That's not to suggest that you'll end up like the lawyer in *Regarding Henry* (Hollywood's stereotypical depiction of a New York lawyer who must suffer a brain injury before he can be transformed from a malevolent narcissist into a decent person), but accidents, crimes, and injuries can happen to lawyers, not just the parties they represent. Luckily, certain types of insurance coverage can buffer the financial strain when they do.

HEALTH INSURANCE

Regardless of age, you need health insurance. It is important to financial stability. Some employers are transitioning employees from employer-administered health plans to the Affordable Care Act's private exchanges. A $95 penalty, or 1 percent of household income, whichever is higher, applies for unenrolled status. "Affordable" is subject to varying definitions. For example, smokers will pay up to 50 percent more than nonsmokers for coverage.

AFFORDABLE CARE ACT

The UC Berkeley Labor Center's calculator estimates costs at http://laborcenter.berkeley.edu/healthpolicy/calculator/.

Tax credit eligibility information is available at IRS.gov/aca.

A menu of private plans through the exchanges is available at www.healthcare.gov. Concerning the potential for penalty, economists' opinions vary, though it is estimated that roughly 55 percent of Americans are likely already in compliance because they have insurance through their employers and/or are covered through Medicare.

Should you simply be unable to afford the premiums, search for a policy with a very high deductible to limit your financial exposure. An example of a high deductible is $5,000. However, even with the rising costs of health insurance, group plans through an employer are generally the cheapest option. If you're fortunate to be young and healthy, a local insurance agent may be able to find you something cheaper with insurance companies that factor age when setting rates. However, be sure to ask what proportion of the premiums collected is actually allocated to pay claims. If the number isn't available in writing, it's usually because up to 50 percent of the premiums collected don't go to pay claims.

When you reach age 55, group coverage is available through AARP (formerly the American Association of Retired Persons). Should insurers deem you uninsurable because of your health history, you may be able to buy health insurance through a state's risk pool.

HMO versus PPO

Most employer group health plans will be either an HMO or a PPO plan. HMOs are the most prevalent form of managed care. In managed care, all health services and financing go through one organization. Services include inpatient and outpatient care and prescription drug benefits. The HMO requires insured members to use its network of hospitals and health care professionals. These health care professionals are either employed by or under contract to the HMO. Members pay a monthly fee that changes only if the entire fee structure changes annually, regardless of the care they may need. PPOs are less restrictive than HMOs. A PPO consists of a group of hospitals and health care professionals who agree to provide care to members at a reduced cost. The benefit of a PPO is flexibility for its members, who do not have to use the services within the network, yet the costs encourage them to do so. Staying within the network means that your costs are lower. When members seek medical care outside the network, they are still covered but must pay a higher deductible and contribute a higher co-payment. Be sure you know what each system offers so you can estimate your actual health care costs.

If your health care options include the choice between an HMO and a PPO, you will need to determine whether your physicians participate and, if not, whether you will be able to afford your share of their fee if you opt for a PPO. The value of continuity in using a physician you've seen for years may provide for more secure diagnoses and would favor paying for outside-the-network medical care. A health maintenance organization (HMO) and a preferred provider organization (PPO) are both managed care plans. Each may monitor and sometimes limit the services and care that its physicians provide to members. Thus, the headline-generating controversy: managed care plans may determine that the medical treatment a member's physician recommends is unnecessary and expensive, resulting in denial of a claim. This means that because both HMOs and PPOs are managed care plans, do not make the mistake of thinking that because your doctor recommends a procedure, the insurer automatically will pay for it. It's not uncommon for an insurer to, in effect, second-guess a doctor and deem a treatment too expensive, ineffective, or unnecessary. That's not to say you can't do your research, fight the insurer's decision, and possibly win. However, it is another reason supporting the establishment of an emergency fund, discussed in Chapters 1 and 2, before indulging in, pampering yourself with,or splurging on "wanted" but not "needed" items.

Nevertheless, if you are fortunate to have a choice between an HMO and a PPO, take time to evaluate the coverage offered by each, and determine which best suits the needs of you and your family.

> Erin prefers a PPO because of a medical condition that requires specialized care and because PPO members do not need a referral before seeing a specialist. However, for Nate, ongoing out-of-pocket costs are his primary concern, so an HMO is a better choice because there are no deductibles and co-payments are typically lower.

COBRA and HIPAA

Should you lose your job, make sure to notify your employer (or your spouse's employer) within 60 days of your intention to elect COBRA benefits so that you can continue your health insurance benefits. Familiarize yourself with what is considered a "qualifying event" under the Consolidated Omnibus Budget Reconciliation Act of 1986 (COBRA), and when coverage can end. (If you lose your job for cause or misconduct, COBRA is inapplicable.) The Health Insurance Portability and Accountability Act of 1996 (HIPAA) may also come into play should there be a preexisting condition issue with your health history. Also, read your employer's Summary Plan Description and plan booklets that spell out the coverage and your rights and responsibilities.

DISABILITY INSURANCE

Group disability insurance coverage is usually available through your employer for a minimal cost. Paid with pretax dollars, it may offer short- or long-term disability coverage to keep your income stream going when you are unable to work due to illness or injury. Disability coverage is measured in time. An insurer will scrutinize an injury or illness, asking whether the policyholder will be back to work in six months, a year, or never. Coverage may kick in (a) the moment your illness or injury renders you temporarily or permanently disabled, or (b) months after you've been diagnosed with a temporary or permanent disability. Route (a) will carry the most expensive premium but offers the best coverage. Defining "disabled" as the inability to do your regular work versus doing *any* work is the policy you want to find, though you may not have much choice if you're buying disability insurance through a group plan offered by your employer.

Whether to purchase a different policy or an additional backup policy independent of your employer depends on (1) the language of your employer's group disability policy in defining "disabled"[1] and how it pays benefits (i.e., percentage

1. Group disability policies tend to have a liberal definition of "disabled" for the first two years; then, insurers tend to become more restrictive with definitions limiting your disabled status to whether you are unable to perform *a* job, as opposed to *your* job. If you can be gainfully employed in some sense, the insurer may likely challenge your disabled status. So, ask for a copy of the policy from your employer and understand the applicable restrictions so you know whether to obtain additional coverage along

of your paycheck, short term or long term, the elimination period); (2) your health history and lifestyle; and (3) family obligations. Long-term disability policies pay benefits for several years or until the age of 65. Short-term policies pay benefits for a shorter period, usually six weeks to two years. The shorter the elimination period and the longer the benefit period, the higher the premium. A standard policy will replace 60 percent of your income, up to a maximum of $5,000 to $10,000 per month.

An important tax consideration is that if you pay your own disability premiums and subsequently become disabled, the disability payments are not taxable. However, if the premiums are paid by your employer, then you will be taxed on the benefits. Should the employer's policy not cover your expenses, then it's usually a good idea to purchase a policy on your own that will allow you to be made financially whole, instead of experiencing a shortfall in earnings, should you be unable to work because a medical condition, illness, or injury renders you disabled. Inquire about a "wraparound" policy for the group disability coverage with your employer, or find another carrier to provide a policy that will provide the full benefits you need.

> Jack earned a $130,000 salary. At the insistence of his well-intentioned albeit nagging mother, he signed up for the group disability policy. It limited his benefits to $5,000 per month ($60,000 per year). His budget fixed expenses at $75,000 a year. To cover the $15,000 gap, he wrapped an individual policy around the group coverage so there would be no shortage in his income stream if he became disabled. His mother had keen foresight when, after a fall on the ski slope, he experienced excruciating back pain so severe it required two separate surgeries, disabling him for nearly 24 months.

If you think you don't need the extra expense of a disability policy, consider that according to the Social Security Administration, a 20-something worker has a 30 percent chance of becoming disabled before retirement. For a 30-year-old, the risk is 4.1 times more likely than death. Still skeptical? You can calculate your potential for becoming disabled at http://www.whatsmypdq.org and learn ways to reduce disability risks at http://www.disabilitycanhappen.org/reducing_chances.

---

with researching other companies (independent of your employer's group insurer) that will provide coverage when your income drops because of disability.

The bottom line: the greatest asset you have is your ability to produce income. Insure it just as you would any other valuable.

LIFE INSURANCE

If you have a child or significant other who is financially dependent upon your income, buy life insurance. Otherwise, save your money. When deciding how much life insurance to buy, the general rule is that you'll need between five and ten times your annual salary. For a more exact calculation, ask yourself these questions: (1) How much of my annual income will my heirs need to replace me? For most, the answer is 75 percent of your annual take-home pay, as opposed to 100 percent, because they will no longer have to pay for your food, clothes, and Starbuck's or gadget habit. (2) What is the annual Social Security benefit, if any, my heirs could expect to receive? The gap, if any, between the answers to questions 1 and 2 will be what you want the life insurance to cover. (3) How long will my heirs need to fill the gap? Consider the ages of your heirs when deciding how long the proceeds will have to cover a gap in income. For example, if you have children in school, estimate how much longer they will need financial support. Assuming that your heirs can invest the proceeds at a 3 percent rate of return after taxes and inflation, calculate the amount of coverage needed from the accompanying table.

Multiply the annual income gap by the figure on the right that corresponds to how long your heirs will need to fill the gap.	
5 years	4.7
10 years	9
15 years	12
20 years	15
25 years	18
30 years	20
50 yeasr	26

For example, assuming that your annual take-home pay is $100,000, your heirs can make do with $75,000 and Social Security will put in $15,000 until your children turn 18. To provide an additional $60,000 for ten years would mean $540,000 of coverage. Factor in an additional half-year's salary for funeral expenses, grief-induced leave of employment for your heir(s), and any other concerns for which payment would be needed. Subtract from this amount the salary of your surviving significant other and assets you've accumulated, such as interest, stock dividends, and your retirement account. As a rule of thumb, you should also add in a cushion of $25,000 to $50,000 if you have children. The resulting number is the amount of life insurance coverage to buy.

Next, look for the cheapest, annually renewable term life insurance. Term insurance is not an investment—it offers no cash value—but it has two advantages for 20-, 30-, and 40-somethings. First, it's cheap, and second, you're not locked in. If you ever decide to drop the policy or switch to another, there's no penalty. The disadvantage is that it will become expensive as you get older (because with age, the probability increases that you may actually die and the beneficiaries will expect payment). Term insurance is what most employers offer. It is generally in force only during the period of your employment. Typically, an employer's insurance will cover one to two times your annual salary, though you may be allowed to purchase additional coverage at a group rate that is lower than you would find on your own.

Insurance companies also market whole-life-type products that combine insurance and investments. The argument favoring a whole life policy is that it forces you to save. You pay an extra premium up front when you're young, then, as you age, the amount of coverage your money buys will shrink, with the savings you've built up via the policy expanding to take its place. A disadvantage is that if what you're really looking for is an investment, you're usually better off buying the term insurance and then depositing the excess money you would have been spending for the whole life policy in an IRA or paying off your home mortgage. The sales fees—loaded into the whole life product—can be high in comparison with the rate of return. Another problem with whole life is that most people let the policies lapse, losing the money they've paid in, or incur a large penalty for early withdrawal.[2]

2. If a salesperson argues that term life is a waste of money because only a small percentage of people ever collect, consider that under that logic, it would seem that few people ever collect on car or fire insurance for their home, but it would be irresponsible not to protect your property.

The crucial issue with whole life products is the rate of interest you will be paid on the savings portion, assuming a good low rate on the insurance portion of the policy. To the extent an insurer provides glossy illustrations showing premiums vanishing as money is compounding, consider whether the money is backed by volatile investments in which you ordinarily wouldn't put your hard-earned paycheck. Generally, the premium goes toward the insurance coverage, administrative fees, and the cash value of your investment. Yet, you have no control over how the insurance company invests the cash value, unless it is variable universal life insurance. With variable universal life insurance, consumers can build cash value just as with the whole life product, but are able to manage their own money by investing in a variety of accounts, similar to mutual funds. Variable products can bring certain tax advantages, though they do come with fees. So, careful analysis of whether the tax consequences are beneficial in comparison with the fees charged and rate of return is necessary before committing funds. The bottom line: if you want insurance coverage, buy term insurance. If you want to invest your money, read Chapter 7. Nevertheless, if you're convinced a whole life or variable universal life policy is the way to go, find a fee-only, independent insurance agent, who for a fixed fee will research the various policies and make a recommendation about the one that's best for you. To ensure objectivity, the agent should not be receiving a commission. As with any investment, calculate what the rate of return will be, after taxes, to determine whether a combined insurance/savings product will help you achieve your financial goals.

For all policies, ask the following questions: (1) What expenses are covered? (2) What are the deductibles, co-payments, and stop-loss provisions? (3) What conditions or treatments are covered by the deductible? (4) What is the company's maximum for payments? (5) Are there conditions and services (interior limits within the policy) that aren't covered? (6) Is the plan guaranteed renewable and noncancelable?

LONG-TERM CARE INSURANCE

Health and disability policies may not cover long-term care, such as home health care, nursing home or assisted living facilities, and adult day care. Although long-term care may appear to be for the elderly, young people may find the need if a debilitating illness or accident occurs with no nearby family or financial savings to handle the care responsibilities.[3] In short, the longer you live, the more likely you'll need long-term care. According to a *New England Journal of Medicine* report, 10 percent of men and 18 percent of women may need nursing home care for one to five years. For obvious reasons, the younger you are, the more likely you are to qualify for benefits. Opting for fewer benefits or a shorter benefit waiting period may trim premium costs, as well as extending the elimination (waiting) period or increasing the deductible. Also, it is worth mentioning that if a couple buys two policies, some companies will waive the premium for the second policy once benefits for the first policy activate. However, at this stage of your career, if handling the basic living expenses is proving difficult, adding long-term care insurance payments is likely not advisable.

PRODUCTS TO AVOID

Don't buy credit life or cancer insurance. It's nearly always cheaper to purchase one comprehensive, all-purpose policy. Also, be cautious of rate structures that (1) offer incredibly low first-year rates, yet have high rates thereafter; and (2) look great, but may be raised at the discretion of the insurer. If you're healthy and enjoy taking a risk, "reversionary term" offers good rates for those in good health; however, the insured will be required to requalify every five years or less. Should your health deteriorate, the insurer may insure you, but at higher rates. You, of course, are free to seek a better rate elsewhere should your health deteriorate, but the danger is that the new insurer's preexisting condition clause may bar coverage for the very illness or condition you want insured.

PROPERTY INSURANCE

If you own a car or home, you have to insure it. The trick is to not overpay for coverage and to ensure that you have sufficient coverage before an accident, fire, or flood occurs.

3. It should be noted that Medicare is not a long-term option because it does not cover custodial care expenses.

Insuring Your Car

How much insurance you must buy often depends on the state you live in. The majority of states require that drivers purchase at least the state's minimum bodily injury liability, which will pay your medical bills and lost wages, along with the medical bills of others hurt in an accident that you are shown to have caused, and property damage up to whatever limits you choose. For example, some states require at least 20/40/10. (The first number equals the bodily injury liability maximum for one person injured in an accident, the second number is the bodily injury liability maximum for all injuries in one accident, and the third number is for the property damage liability maximum for one accident.) A 20/40/10 requirement translates to $20,000 of coverage per person, $40,000 of coverage for more than one person, and $10,000 for property damage. Personal injury or medical coverage pays your own medical costs if you're injured in an accident. It is recommended that unless you have no assets, you should at least have limits of 100/300 for bodily injury to sufficiently cover your medical costs and possible lost wages.

The Internet is a great resource for comparing rates and locating the best deal in your region. Check the deductibles and don't pay for unnecessary extras. For example, collision coverage pays for repairing your car if you hit something, so don't buy it if you have a beat-up clunker. Likewise, when you have good health insurance, medical coverage may not be necessary. Nevertheless, if you have assets to protect, buy enough liability insurance to do so. When you have a good driving record, you may be able to significantly lower your premium by accepting a high deductible of $500–$1,000.

Insuring Your Home

Shop around for the best rates and consider the deductibles. Do insure your home for at least 80 percent of its replacement cost (because even partial losses will not be considered fully covered). Review your policy every year to ensure that you aren't paying for more (or less) coverage than needed. To the extent you would have to rebuild your home if it were completely destroyed, be sure that you increase the limits as the cost associated with home building increases. This can be done through an inflation rider, which will increase the coverage annually at the rate of inflation. Also, do add $1 million in liability insurance for slips and falls (because chances are when your new neighbor learns that you are one of those high-priced lawyers, he will ask for pain and suffering incurred from falling on your porch while dropping off your welcome neighbor basket).

"Replacement cost coverage" will increase the premium, but it is usually worth it. This is because if your high-definition TV is stolen, you'll want to replace it with a new one, versus "actual cash value," which will only pay the cost of the TV when you first purchased it. List all valuables, such as jewelry, antiques, silverware, and the like, that you want covered in a schedule attached to the policy. If you have a business-related office set up at home, your homeowners (or renters) policy likely won't cover a stolen computer or scanner without a special endorsement for it. So, ask your agent for a separate quote. Also, some insurers offer discounts for precautionary measures such as smoke detectors, fire extinguishers, deadbolts, or alarm systems. Finally, homeowners insurance does not cover land, so when deciding how much to purchase, exclude the land value from your calculation.

Flood insurance should be considered when your home is located near water or could be considered "near water" once in a great while. Typically, flood insurance requires that a full year's premium be paid up to five days in advance before coverage will be in effect. Unless the home is sold, cancellation will not be permitted mid-year (as in when the home survives the rainy season unscathed).

> Conduct an annual review of your homeowners insurance, confirming that (1) the specific features of the policy are right for you; (2) you're including everything that you need to for coverage; (3) the amount of insurance is sufficient given any changes in your status in life and the value of your property; and (4) the policy is priced competitively for what if offers.

Umbrella Policy

An umbrella policy is essentially extended personal liability coverage. If your liability policy stops at $500,000 but the accident victim sues you for $1 million, the umbrella policy comes into play. It covers almost any noncriminal activity you could be sued for that is unrelated to your business or profession. For example, Clark Griswold needed an umbrella policy when an elderly uncle's simple act of lighting a cigar near Clark's brittle tree set the uncle on fire in the movie *Christmas Vacation*. Even though it seems unlikely that you'll ever need the shelter of an umbrella policy, if you have assets to protect, you should buy this as supplemental coverage—at least a million dollars' worth of personal liability coverage. Under certain circumstances, some umbrella policies will kick in where an insured's auto liability policy stopped. As with all contracts, read the fine print to understand the restrictions before buying.

> When a guest unfortunately drowned in Jeff's backyard swimming pool, an umbrella policy alleviated the financial consequences.

Renters Insurance

If you have valuables that you can't afford to replace if they were lost or stolen, you should buy renters insurance.

INSURING CHILDREN

Don't bother. Life insurance is to replace the income earned by the policyholder so that any financial strain is eliminated or at least lessened for the policyholder's dependents. Unless you have income-producing children or your children have dependents, they don't need life insurance. The money can be put toward one of your other financial goals.

DEDUCTIBLES

When comparing insurance premiums for the best deal, ask what you would save by opting for the highest deductible. With respect to property, the big risks are the ones you want to be protected against—destruction of your home by fire, for example—not the little ones. So, a higher deductible may be worth the risk and cost-analysis. With respect to your health, whether a high deductible is best depends on your individual circumstances. If you're young and healthy, you may be able to afford a higher deductible. However, if you have a family member who is prone to illness, the higher deductible will cause you to incur significant out-of-pocket expenses.

HEALTH SAVINGS ACCOUNTS (HSAS)

The Medicare Prescription Drug, Improvement, and Modernization Act of 2003 set up HSAs for qualified medical expenses. HSAs are like an IRA for medical expenses—an eligible individual who is covered under a high-deductible health plan can contribute the amount of the annual deductible on a tax-deductible basis. Distributions can be made at any time so long as they are for qualified medical expenses. HSAs make high-deductible medical plans a cheaper alternative and are worth researching for eligibility and compatibility with your particular circumstances.

INVENTORY

Take an inventory of your household belongings, along with photos or video of everything, so you'll have a readily available way to prove your losses should there be a fire or other damage. A fireproof safe or safety-deposit box in a safe location is appropriate for storing the insurance inventory and accompanying photos/video.

TO FILE OR NOT TO FILE

Insurers will likely raise your rates and charge higher premiums if you file claims, regardless of whether the damage caused was your fault. It may seem an unfair punishment, but that's the way it is. Remember, you're really buying insurance coverage to protect from catastrophic losses that pose a financial disaster. So, before you file a claim, consider whether it is small enough that you can cover it out-of-pocket versus risking a higher premium at year's end or, in some circumstances, a refusal by the insurer to renew your policy altogether.

> Andrea accidentally hit a deer while driving. It caused substantial damage to her car, and she filed a claim. The following month when hail cracked her windshield, she opted to pay for the damage out-of-pocket rather than risk a raise in her rates by the insurer.

THE FICO SCORE PRACTICE

Although a few states prohibit auto and home insurers from using credit scoring formulas to help determine premiums, the controversial practice continues elsewhere. The reason is that researchers have found a correlation between how well people handle credit and how likely they are to cost the insurer money. The presumption is that a high credit score translates to the fewest claims filed. Thus, if your credit history is shaky, an insurer may deem you more likely to file claims, and you will pay higher premiums.

OTHER INSURANCE

Dental coverage is usually not part of your health insurance policy. Dental care may be purchased as a rider to the main policy, however. If not, you can obtain an individual dental policy. Rental car insurance may not be necessary if you already have car insurance. Verify with your insurance agent to what extent you are covered if you rent a car. Regarding travel insurance, if your schedule is subject to change or you are planning foreign travel, insurance can be worth the investment. Buy from an independent company as opposed to a travel or tour agency. Read the fine print because certain events or items may be excluded. Speaking of fine print, pet insurance is seldom a good deal because of the exclusions that a standard policy usually contains, especially concerning specialized treatments.

TAKING CARE OF YOUR HEALTH

The best protection for your health is implementing good health habits now. Every dollar spent on medical expenses is a dollar that is not going toward your goals. Learn whether it's time for a change to your health habits at http://www.realage.com.

If you need further incentive, consider that practicing healthy habits also protects your most important asset as a lawyer: the brain. Sandra Bond Chapman, PhD, founder and chief director of the Center for BrainHealth at The University of Texas at Dallas, Dee Wyly Distinguished University Chair, and author of *Make*

Your Brain Smarter, is committed to maximizing cognitive potential across the entire lifespan. As a cognitive neuroscientist with more than 40 funded research grants, Dr. Chapman elucidates and applies novel approaches to advance creative and critical thinking, strengthen healthy brain development, and incite innovation throughout life. She shared her insights in the following interview.

Q. What actions can busy professionals take now to protect their brains from unnecessary cognitive decline (e.g., attempting to stave off dementia and/or Alzheimer's for as long as possible)?

A. Practicing healthy brain habits daily is essential for present and long-term brain health. The earlier we start and more fully committed we are to a brain healthy lifestyle, the more successful we will be at building a resilient and vibrant brain capable of staving off Alzheimer's. At the Center for BrainHealth, we have developed scientifically proven strategies to enhance brain performance, improve brain efficiency, and strengthen overall brain health.

Decades of cognitive neuroscience research reveal that the brain is wired to think critically, synthesize information, and develop innovative solutions. The good news is that, as an attorney, you have chosen a challenging career path that can give your brain the mental exercise that it needs to thrive. To maximize this professional brain benefit, don't let yourself fall into rote thinking that creates routine work products and boring meetings without forward progress. Instead, constantly challenge yourself to think deeper, consider new perspectives, and create new pithy but powerful bottom-line messages to convey key points in fresh ways. Also, carefully mentor young attorneys so they can become generalized strategic thinkers—a greater asset to the firm and to their own continued brain health. The brain is built by how it is used every single day. If young attorneys are primarily expected to be fact-finders, they will have difficulty stepping into the role of high-level synthesizers from research relevant to the problem to be solved.

On the other hand, some downsides to the legal profession often include grueling work hours and seemingly unmanageable amounts of information to consume and process, which has deleterious effects on the brain.

To combat this hectic pace, one of the most important commitments you can make to yourself is to eliminate toxic habits such as multitasking and constant mental work. Yes, the old adage "use it or lose it" is outdated. We are using our brains so hard we are burning them out—leaving us feeling completely brain-depleted at the end of the day. And we are. It is time to stop. As a busy professional, this drastic change in brain habits may seem counterintuitive, but the results will actually boost your productivity [and] quality of work and add to your mental longevity—on a daily and lifelong basis.

Brainpower of One: Your brain is wired to do one task at a time. In fact, when you believe you are multitasking you are actually switching quickly from one task to the next, placing undo strain on the brain. To combat this often engrained lifestyle hazard, become a *sequential-tasker*. Make a practice of silencing phones [and] e-mail alerts and shutting your door when dealing with tasks of substance.

Brainpower of Two: Reserve prime brain time on your calendar for the most critical items that require the deepest thinking on your to-do list. Know what your top two critical accomplishments are each day and execute them before letting yourself be distracted by smaller items on your to-do list.

Brainpower of None: Your brain works best when you allow it to work behind the scenes, but it can't do that if you are constantly monopolizing it with nonstop mental work. Practice a five by five principle. Give yourself at least five minutes, five times a day to sit back or step away from the daily grind and give your brain the downtime it needs to reset and reinvigorate for your next aha moment.

Q. From reading articles on the Center's website, it appears that the Center's research includes studying the impact of addictions, stroke, and other physical ailments on one's cognitive functions. Presuming that the goal is to operate at maximum cognitive efficiency so that one can be productive—whether that's productive in the workplace or productive in completing the tasks of daily living—do you have examples of dietary changes [or] mental or physical exercises that

busy professionals [can] incorporate in their day-to-day activities to stave off dementia and, in turn, avoid (or at least delay) the need for incurring caregiving assistance expenses?

A. Until recently, cognitive decline in healthy adults was viewed as inevitable. Our findings indicate that the benefits of cognitive exercise generalize to more areas of brain health than aerobic exercise. Just 12 hours of directed brain training over a 12-week time period revealed individuals retooled their mental work habits and were able to experience significant brain changes across widespread networks that support independent high-level thinking throughout life. Some of the significant gains in brain health included major increases in regional and global brain blood flow, 30 percent faster speed of neural communication, and increased white matter—the wiring that carries the messages across brain regions. Our brain is like a bank account. The more cognitive power we add to our personally specific cognitive endowment on a regular basis, the more these reserves will help us to protect against cognitive losses.

While a study that focused on physical exercise also produced impressive results, the improvements were more limited than the gains from synthesized mental workouts. Nonetheless, physical exercise significantly improved both immediate and delayed memory (holding on to information like a phone number ~25 minutes later) without having to spend extra time practicing memory tricks to remember. Delayed memory is one of the earliest symptoms of Alzheimer's; so exercise may be able to increase the number of years with higher memory function.

Using your brain strategically by practicing the [preceding] outlined strategies . . . (Brainpower of None, One, and Two) and engaging in complex thinking are two of the best gifts you can give your brain. Other great brain supporters include regular exercise (at least 30 minutes, three to four times a week), a heart healthy diet, and getting seven to eight hours of sleep a night.

Q. Procrastination in making a plan for one's retirement and procrastination in improving one's health have been hurdles for many people to conquer. Do you have any suggestions or tips for busy professionals

to do to try to retrain their brains out of procrastination mode and into focusing on making a plan for retirement and/or health improvements (e.g., exercise, diet, etc.)?

A. Procrastinating over important decisions wastes time and increases stress levels that detrimentally impact cognitive function. Taking the bull by the horns and making yourself set personal goals allows more time for pleasurable activities. Becoming and remaining a strategic thinker is one of the best ways to deter procrastination. A non-tactical thinker spends [an] inordinate amount of time on busywork without making the big things happen. Crucial elements to boost personal satisfaction [and] brain energy and keep a forward momentum include maintaining cognitive brain health, staying engaged in personal decisions, and continually building rich life experiences.

Follow these steps to avoid procrastination:

1. Create a "to do" list.
2. Prioritize items most important to you.
3. Once you identify the most important items, break them down into a series of individual tasks.
4. Get advice on the items that you don't want to spend hours getting up to speed on; you do not have to be an expert in all matters—that can be a brain drain. Pick where you spend your mental energy.
5. Set a deadline; put a date for completion on each task.
6. Give yourself a small reward for completing each task.
7. Give yourself a bigger reward when you complete the final task or make the final decision.

Q. Are there adverse effects of sleep deprivation on the brain?

A. Sleep is arising as one of the key factors that contribute to brain health. Current research is developing biomarkers that attest to sleep deprivation's detrimental effects. A good night's sleep cleans out toxins in your brain, lets your brain consolidate information at deeper levels, and can settle emotions from the day before and sets the stage for a mentally productive day. Many individuals have their greatest breakthrough thoughts in the middle of sleep because our brain keeps working for us and free associates to generate new ways of seeing situations like a complex case.

Losing even a couple of nights of adequate sleep puts you in a state that resembles jet lag or even early dementia causing memory and concentration problems and can require at least ten days to fully recover. Pulling all-nighters to finish a brief is like a double whammy—depleting benefits and making your brain feel foggy. Tip: When you are under the gun during a big case, make sleep a major priority. Sleep is critical for keeping your mind sharp and productive. If six to eight hours is unrealistic, aim for at least five hours during your regular sleep cycle. If all else fails, even a 30-minute nap can help the brain rebound.

In sum, insurance is a way of transferring risk. How much risk you should retain and how much should be transferred to an insurance company is a personal decision. Consider the degree of risk you're able to tolerate, the likelihood of the risk affecting you, and the cost of transferring the risk. As always, check all contractual language, making certain the policy covers you more like a blanket as opposed to swiss cheese with holes where coverage should apply. Even if your initial reaction is to dismiss coverage because you are young and healthy, when you have children or other loved ones who are financially dependent on your income, it is financially irresponsible not to purchase disability, health, and life insurance.

Chapter 7

Investment Basics

Index funds are going to beat the results of most investors.

—Warren Buffett

Buy low and sell high; you've heard the adage, but if financial success were that simplistic, everyone who owns stock would automatically be a multimillionaire. The fact is that you're unlikely to conquer Wall Street by individual buy-and-sell stock picks. To do so, you would have to spend the time equivalent to that of an analyst, a researcher, and a trader combined (and, if you have that much free time on your hands at your job, you're either going to be laid off or fired, so you shouldn't be putting any money in the stock market).

MANAGING A PORTFOLIO

Successful management of your investment portfolio is based on four fundamentals: (1) diversifying assets; (2) minimizing costs and taxes; (3) outpacing inflation; and (4) buying and holding for the long term. For rookie investors, add a fifth element: stock index funds. Study after study has shown that stock index funds outperform the average investor and even some mutual fund managers. In short, stock index funds are your best bet for long-term investing success.

DIVERSIFICATION

Unless you love risk, diversification is essential. It balances the ups and downs of the market in an effort to make up for the fact that no one truly knows what the future will bring (hence, the reason it's difficult to know if you're buying a stock when it's really at its "all-time low" or selling when it's really reached its "all-time high").

PRACTICAL EXAMPLE OF DIVERSIFICATION'S EFFECT

Assume that you had a $100,000 retirement nest egg in the S&P 500 when the stock market dived in 2008. If it was allocated 100 percent in stocks, you lost $37,000, because the S&P's return was −37 percent in 2008. On the other hand, if you had invested in an allocation of 50 percent stock, 50 percent bonds, you would have reduced the risk of loss such that the nest egg would have still taken a hit, but one that was much less. In fact, you would have had a retirement nest egg valued at $84,120 at 2008's end.

To diversify, spread your assets over four categories of investments:

Liquid. This is cash. After you've paid off debt, socked away an emergency fund, and maxed out the annual retirement contribution, put your money in a money market bank account. If you can't meet the minimum for a money market account yet, a bank savings account is fine. It's not sexy, but it's safe, and that's the purpose of this portion. This is money that you can convert to cash quickly, if needed. When will it be needed? When you find an investment that is undervalued, as opposed to overvalued or fairly valued. In the meantime, you won't lose your money. You'll save it and earn interest.

Inflation Defense. Inflation affects the power of your money. It's an important factor in calculating whether you'll have enough money in the future to accomplish your goals, especially retirement, and will be discussed more in Chapter 9. For now, know that it is an important consideration in your investment strategy. If you can afford it, put some money in items that hold their value when paper money does not. A home, gold, silver, or other real estate investments are typical examples. As you probably know, inflation is the result of the government printing more money when in deficit. But don't make the mistake of assuming a deficit's presence will allow you to predict horrendous inflation. Consider the size of the national debt in relation to the economy as a whole. You don't have to be an economist to understand that if the economy grows by 4 percent and the national debt by 4 percent, the national debt is not dangerously bigger, relative to the economy as a whole.

Deflation Defense. Although the analysts and the media focus on inflation, there is a possibility of deflation. Think the 1930s when things were cheap, but no one had any money to buy anything. Cash and a 30-year Treasury bond are the best examples of a deflation hedge. So, the "liquid money" portion of your investment can double as a deflation defense, too. The way the bond works is that you're locking in a certain rate for 30 years (e.g., 8 percent for 30 years; if the going rate drops to 3 percent, you're deemed the new "It" market watcher).

Affluence Hedge. When a prosperous economy reigns, you want to be in on it, and the stock market provides you with the potential opportunity. Notice the word "potential." Essentially, the stock market is legalized gambling. It is not for short-term cash or money you can't afford to lose. For example, if you're planning to buy a home in three to five years, don't put the down payment money in the stock market. For amateurs, the best investment vehicle is a no load (no sales commission), stock index fund. Invest as much as you can comfortably afford to part with monthly. You can arrange a monthly electronic transfer to your fund account of a specified amount after you receive your paycheck, just as you can with your money market or savings account.

SELECTING AN ASSET ALLOCATION

Asset allocation involves determining how much money you want in each of the four categories of investment. "Don't put all your eggs in one basket." That's the theory behind diversification, and that's how asset allocation works. When one sector has low returns,[1] the other should have high returns; diversification

1. A "return" on investments can be income, capital appreciation, or both. For example, assume you buy a stock for $100. After a year, it produces $8 in dividends. The income return would be $8 divided by $100 = 8 percent, or the current yield. If at the end of the next year, the stock is worth $112, it has appreciated by 12 percent (12/100); this is the growth rate. The total return is 20 percent, the sum of the income return and growth rate (8 percent + 12 percent).

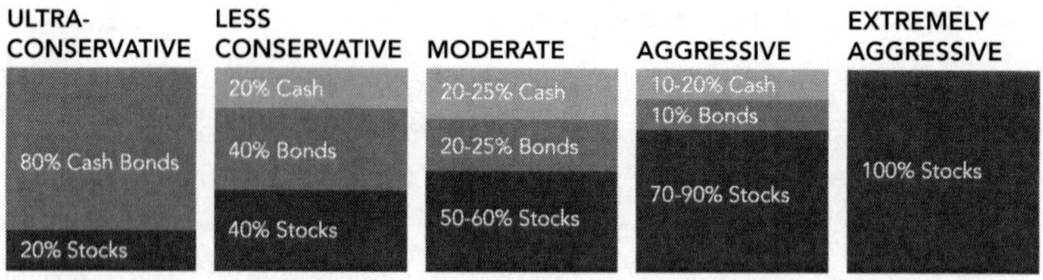

ensures a balance so a single downturn won't financially wipe you out. Cash, stocks, bonds, mutual funds, and cash equivalents (e.g., Treasury bills, CDs) will make up a diversified portfolio. Tolerance for risk, age, life events, how much time you have before you'll need the money, the current status of the market, interest rate decreases/increases, and predictions for the future are factors that will help you choose from ultraconservative to extremely aggressive allocations. Generally, stocks have the highest return and highest risk,[2] bonds offer lower returns and lower risk, and money market accounts are the lowest return and lowest risk.

Different types of investments behave differently. For this reason, when you conduct your annual review of your finances, discussed in Chapters 1 and 2, consider whether to reallocate your investments once a year as well as when there is a significant change in the economy. For example, if your stocks had a fantastic year, but bonds were sluggish, you might decide to change to a more aggressive allocation with an increase in the stock allocation. Another practical example is that if bonds did well, but you anticipate that interest rates will rise, increasing the bond allocation would be a mistake. Don't buy bonds when it is anticipated that interest rates will rise because you'll be saddled with a lower than market rate and earning less than if you had waited.

2. *Highest risk investments* include futures, commodities, limited partnerships, collectibles, real estate investment trusts (REITs), penny stocks, speculative stocks (i.e., stock in new companies), and high-yield (junk) bonds. (Note: "high yield" does not mean high interest with little risk.) *Moderate risk investments* include growth stocks (companies that reinvest most of their profits), corporate bonds with low ratings, balanced mutual funds, aggressive mutual funds, rental real estate, annuities, and international stocks. *Limited risk investments* are corporate and municipal bonds with high ratings, index mutual funds, and blue-chip stocks (i.e., Dow Jones). The investments are measured against the particular index to which they apply. The Standard & Poors (S&P 500) is the index for 500 of the largest companies in America, and the Russell 2000 measures the performance of small- to mid-cap companies, for example.

THE FINANCIAL INDUSTRY'S RULE OF THUMB: SUBTRACT 110 OR 120 FROM YOUR AGE

It used to be that to calculate how much money you should allocate to stocks and bonds, the financial industry recommended subtracting your age from 100; the result is the stock or equities allocation. Because of the longevity trend among Americans, the financial industry now suggests subtracting 110 or 120 from your age to see what the allocation should be for stock investments. The theory is that if you're living longer, you need to earn extra growth that stocks can provide.

Typically, the younger you are, the greater your financial ability to handle more risk, presuming you have the stomach for it and don't plan on retiring at 30-something. For example, when you're in your 20s, allocating up to 90 percent to stocks or stock mutual funds is generally appropriate presuming that the other factors (risk tolerance, time before you need the money, state of the market, and interest rates) fall into place. In your 30s, you may choose a less aggressive position at 70 to 80 percent stocks or stock mutual funds, and adding bonds for stability and income, again depending on the other factors. When you have limited funds to diversify and need to stretch them over the four categories previously discussed, consider that cash will cover liquidity and deflation. Convertible bonds can provide a fair fixed income in the event of deflation (unless the issuer goes broke), and the value of the bond rises if the common stock (into which it's convertible) rises, such as during periods of moderate inflation or prosperity. Likewise, U.S. savings bonds can be relatively liquid, provide a guaranteed rate of interest (which proves good in the event of deflation), and provide for a possibility of high interest (during inflation).

Importantly, if you anticipate needing to use your money in less than five years (such as for a down payment on a home), the stock market is not the best option. Rather, investing your money in lower-risk vehicles, such as short-term bond funds or federally insured CDs, would be better.

DIGITAL CURRENCY

Although still experimental, the digital currency market has achieved mainstream appeal since Greece blocked depositors from their bank accounts.

The U.S. government's acknowledgment of digital currencies via regulations means that transactions in bitcoin must follow the same rules that all other currencies do. Intended as a global currency, it can be especially useful in countries where citizens do not have easy access to banks, because bitcoin is transferred peer-to-peer. It is not backed by a government or bank; rather, individuals trade, sell, and invest in it. If you accepted bitcoin as an alternative currency from a client when it was worth pennies and held on to it, you've seen the price soar past more than $800, then drop and hover, then increase again. A downside of digital currencies such as bitcoin is that a currency is only as good as what it can be used to do. Bitcoin and other digital currencies still have kinks to work out, including the market in which you can use bitcoin to buy and sell goods and services. Before jumping on the digital currencies bandwagon, research it. Bitcoin, for example, has been a roller-coaster ride of extreme price fluctuations, and its price fluctuates by the second. Again, digital currencies such as bitcoin are still experimental. So, the first rule of investing applies: if you cannot afford to lose the money, do not invest it. That being said, if you have the funds to risk on experimenting, the Bitcoin Foundation website can provide additional resources and information at https://bitcoinfoundation.org.

MINIMIZING TAXES AND COSTS

Calculate the net rate of return of an investment. That's the return after the IRS, traders, and financial advisors take their cuts of the transaction. Calculating the net return helps you minimize taxes and costs. Most fund managers' estimates set an average rate of return at 8 percent, before fees, taxes, and inflation. Never initiate a transaction without analyzing tax consequences and the costs and fees. Unlike other aspects of investing, taxes and costs are actually something within your control. Tax consequences include short-term capital gains (positions sold in less than one year), long-term capital gains (positions sold after more than one year), dividends, and deferred capital gains (eventual sale of fund shares); the most expensive of these is short-term capital gains. To avoid taking a hit on short-term gains, you either never sell winning stocks and/or funds held for less than a year, or always offset short-term gains with short-term losses. It is the failure to follow this rule that destroys the after-tax performance of many mutual funds, including hedge funds.

Industry standard factors a tax bite of up to 2 percent. However, exact taxes are subjectively determined by the transaction and the investor's particular financial situation. Costs and fees of portfolio management and transactions vary according to the particular advisor and services offered. Expect a 0.2 percent annual fee for a globally diversified index fund of 60 percent stocks and 40 percent bonds. One-on-one, independent advisor fees range from 0.25 to 0.50 percent. Trading fees are additional.

GETTING INTO THE MARKET VIA MUTUAL FUNDS

Mutual funds are the easiest way to invest. Mutual funds invest in stocks and bonds of many different companies. They are lower risk than if you were picking individual stocks and bonds on your own. Starting deposit amounts vary; some may require up to $3,000, and others much less. Likewise, some mutual funds are riskier than others, and different funds have different investing objectives, such as income, growth, or tax management.

Load versus No Load

"Load" is the fee charged by the fund and is stated as a percentage of the amount purchased or sold. Front-end (pay up front) and back-end (pay when you sell) loads will eat into your profits, which is why no-load funds are more attractive. The benefits of no-load funds are that they offer diversification, professional management, and economies of scale at minimal cost. The fund pools your money with that of others and invests the resulting millions according to its guidelines published in its prospectus. Stocks, bonds, domestic, international, high risk, low risk, tax-free, or taxable: it's all available. No sales commission (no load) or back-end redemption fee is charged. When choosing what funds to invest in, ignore the following: (a) those that charge more than 1 percent a year in advisory, administrative, or marketing fees; (b) specialized funds that invest only in a particular sector of the economy, such as gold or technology, unless you believe that you can outguess the fund manager; and (c) funds that will complement your objectives (e.g., long-term growth, tax-free).

Types of Mutual Funds

A summary of the advantages and disadvantages of certain types of funds follows.

Index. Proper diversification requires 20 to 30 different stocks. You would likely have to read prospectuses and annual reports on 200 to 300 stocks to pick 20 to 30 winners, and most individual investors don't have the time (or knowledge) needed to do the necessary research. This is why index funds are best for amateurs as well as for those investors who don't have time to spend keeping up with the financial research necessary to track companies and who don't want to pay a manager to pick stocks. Study after study has established that actively managed, conventional-type mutual funds often underperform the stock market. This is another reason a stock index mutual fund is beneficial. An index fund's objective is to match the return of a specified index by buying shares in each stock in that index; the fund tries to replicate the market, whether it's the Standard & Poor's 500 or indexes tracking a single industry or overseas market. Index funds also charge lower fees than actively managed funds. Finally, buying an index fund is almost always a better after-tax choice than buying a conventional mutual fund or hedge fund, discussed next.

Hedge. The goal of hedge funds is to make money right now by active trading. Taxwise, this means hedge funds will rack up short-term gains. Thus, the more you or your fund manager trade, the more you have to beat your benchmark to just break even. Hedge fund managers generally charge two fees—management (which usually exceeds 1 percent) and incentive (typically set at 20 percent or more of net profits)—versus traditional investments in which only a management fee is charged. High-water marks provide that if the fund loses money, the investors pay only the management fee. However, there is nothing to prevent a manager from quitting instead of working without incentive compensation should the fund fall below its high-water mark. Fund managers, at their core, have the fun (and stress) of gambling with other people's money. Because hedge funds have traditionally been a vehicle reserved for the uber-rich, if your money is invited to participate in one, congrats! However, proceed with caution. As with all other investment opportunities, research the fund management, where your money is going, the tax consequences, and the rate of return.

Conventional. These actively managed funds employ managers and teams of research analysts whose goal is to pick stocks of companies that will outperform their peers. The expense of employing these people increases costs, which, in turn, reduces fund returns. Most impose fees and other penalties to discourage investors from buying and selling shares quickly, because this is trading activity that can harm long-term shareholders. It should be mentioned that there can be similar charges imposed at discount brokerage firms that distribute funds with "no transaction fee" settings, as well as by full-service brokerages that may charge "contingent deferred sales charges," which apply when you sell certain funds within several years of purchase.

Tax Management. These funds employ a variety of techniques designed to avoid making certain income and capital gain payouts. Do not choose these funds for a "tax-advantaged" account, such as a 401(k), however. The argument for choosing tax management funds over others is that they harvest losses that can be used to offset unavoidable long-term gains and can be more specifically tailored to an investor's specific tax consequences. Critics respond that competent investors will manage their financial life from an after-tax perspective anyway, leaving index funds still the best bet. In fact, several companies have discontinued marketing their tax management funds apparently due to lack of investor interest.

Whether you decide to invest in mutual funds, such as an index fund, or do your own individual stock picks, always analyze the tax consequences. It's the best way to boost your return, and, for those with an addictive personality, calculating tax ratios can help to curb a stock speculation addict's urge to risk profits for the adrenaline rush of buying and selling.

AVOID COMMON MARKET MISTAKES

Whether you are an amateur or a seasoned professional, the financial health of your investments can become derailed if you don't keep the following in mind when considering whether, and how, to invest in the market.

Mania Doesn't Equal Money. It's easy to get sucked into the hype. "Everybody's doing it" wasn't a good justification for your parents to allow you to jump off the roof, and it's not a good reason for investing in something, either. For many, the stock market is a snoozer, and learning about how it ticks generates yawns. Enter the financial media, devoted to helping you make a profit while entertaining you at the same time. Except, they have to make a profit, too, and their way is to make the market entertaining; otherwise, you won't watch, read, or listen.

Tantalizing IPOs, top ten ways to beat the pros, debates about what stocks will be the next Microsoft: the message is the stock market is exciting! Get involved! Move that money! The reality is that once you've mastered the investment basics and have a good financial footing, frenetic account activity is dangerous. Think about it: every time you initiate a transaction, you can incur transaction fees and taxes as well as enduring the psychological stress of wondering whether it will it go up and boring your family and friends by complaining about the market when it goes down. Worse, the financial media's focus in their programs and articles is often short-term thinking. Short-term purchases decrease your odds of making a significant profit. Read any article by, or about, self-made billionaire and investment guru Warren Buffett and you'll learn that the most profitable (and predictable) way of earning money is investing for the long term, not soaking up a financial commentator's short-term stock picks. Long-term equals decades—at least ten years—not months. That's not to say don't read investment articles or listen to and watch the investment shows. They have some good stories: markets soaring or crashing, the latest scams and swindles, underdogs becoming rich or going broke, CEOs doing the perp walk and being marched off to jail. Just keep in mind that bankruptcy, government investigations, fraud, and unbridled success have been part of the market forever—and have even proved a staple for many a lawyer's livelihood! So, don't get too caught up in the entertainment, becoming reactionary without careful scrutiny of what, if anything, lies behind the big story or the next big stock picks.

Advisors and Predictions. True visionaries are rare. There are probably as many predictors, prognosticators, and financial advisors with methods to psych out the market as there are investors. In fact, there's an old Wall Street story about an advisor who is walking near the harbor with a prospective client, pointing out all the yachts owned by the successful brokers. "But, where are all the customers' yachts?" the potential customer innocently asks. Silence. Perhaps the *New York Times*'s 1986 article "Leaving the Law for Wall Street" sums up Wall Street's allure best: there's so much money to be made, it causes lawyers to bolt from law firms to find jobs in the financial mecca. That's not to suggest that all advisors, analysts, or brokers are cloaked in greed, but when someone quips about a sure-fire way to earn a phenomenal return on your money, don't be swayed by the slick brochures or a chart illustrating those projected returns. Projected returns are not fact; they're nothing more than statistics, so treat that advisor like an opponent's expert witness.

Deconstruct that chart like it's exhibit 1 and interrogate the advisor about the underlying information that went into that chart—specifically, the phenomenal rate of return the advisor is promoting. What are the assumptions that went into those projected returns? (Often, there will be no assumptions.) How were the projected returns calculated? Were the projected returns calculated before or after the fees, transactions costs, taxes, and inflation? (The more phenomenal the return, the more likely it was calculated before all of these adjustments.) The goal is to make certain that the data and statistics are not being manipulated to paint a rosier picture than what will likely occur if you invest your money. Moreover, assumptions based on a ten-year average of how an investment has performed is only a snapshot. According to an article coauthored by Warren Buffett for *Fortune* in 2001, during the twentieth century, there were three bull markets in which the Dow jumped more than 11 points and three major stagnant markets in which the Dow lost 292 points. In the aggregate, the three bull markets lasted a total of 44 years; the bear markets, 56 years, leaving more than a century when the Dow's performance was not stellar. The point: it takes decades' worth of information to determine how the market will trend, not a pie chart illustrating projected returns.

Piling On. People think the market is about getting in when a stock is hot or about to soar, then piling everything into it and earning a windfall when you sell in a few months or years. The problem is that predicting the market is notoriously difficult. From hostile takeovers of the '80s to junk bonds, dot-coms, IPOs, and the stock market crash in 2000, and LBOs (leveraged buyouts) in between, bubbles burst. When the bubble bursts on a trend, the ride ends, and it always ends badly. Diversification is the safest way to protect your finances.

> Initially diversified, Alec began investing in dot-coms. His stock investment grew to $1.6 million. Overwhelmed by a money-making frenzy, he ignored diversification principles, believed the media hype, and piled all of his money, including his retirement funds and home savings, onto the dot-com ride. The stock plummeted before he could sell it, and his net worth dropped to $52,000.

Asset Classes. It's important to diversify among different types of investments (cash, stocks, bonds, international stocks), but it can be just as important to diversify within those asset classes. In other words, don't put all your eggs (especially if they are your retirement eggs) in one company's basket. For a cautionary tale, you need look no further than the headlines generated by the former Enron employees who went broke putting their retirement money in one company's stock—Enron. Had they diversified their retirement assets, the financial hit they took when Enron collapsed would not have been as devastating.

Sure Things. A remarkable, self-perpetuating truth of accumulating wealth is that you get invited to put your money in sure things, little-to-no-risk investments, designed to make you wealthier. From family members to friends to hungry financial advisors who read of your new job status—all may call you with an offering of a "sure thing." Whether these are stocks, investment strategies, or entrepreneurial ventures, carefully scrutinize these opportunities just as you would any other, with the four fundamentals of investing: (1) diversifying assets; (2) minimizing costs and taxes; (3) outpacing inflation; and (4) buying and holding for the long term. This is because even if your friend has earned wheelbarrows full of money on an opportunity, it doesn't mean that you will or that the investment is right for the goals you have. Finally, remember the only sure things in life, as Benjamin Franklin said long ago, are death and taxes.

Paying Tax on Someone Else's Gain. In December, mutual funds post their gains and, in turn, pass along their proportionate share of all the capital gains that the funds have realized from selling assets all year. The result: you gain immediate taxable income without increasing your shares' value. The way to escape this scenario is to learn when the fund will post its gain for the year, and then buy your share(s) after that date.

Insider Trading. Don't. The government will eventually catch up to you. Even if you're smart enough not to leave a paper trail, someone always talks (e.g., the person you're in collusion with brags to the wrong person, or a curious observer enviously coveting your unexplainable meteoric financial success anonymously calls in a tip to the feds). No amount of money is worth losing your freedom, family, friends, career, and reputation. The only one who will get rich is the legal team you will have to hire to defend you.

Hiring Help. It's one thing to get advice, but don't trust your money in someone else's hands. When hiring help, understand where your money is going—fees, commissions, back-loads, front-loads—and don't give someone the authority to unilaterally sign checks for you. Licensed financial helpers have different titles: advisor, attorney, CPA, financial planner; whatever the title, if you're hiring someone to give you advice on your financial investments, and manage them, he or she should not be charging more than 1 percent per year of the assets managed. To ensure objectivity, make certain that the advisor is not earning a commission from the companies being recommended to you. There are some fee-only financial advisors or planners, which means they are paid by the hour and are not benefiting from recommending one investment over another. If you are paying on an hourly basis, make certain to learn what and how the financial planner charges before the engagement. Consulting financial advisors can be helpful in complex situations or life events such as a divorce. Although seeking a financial advisor can help you educate yourself about investments, you should do your own research, too. For many, it's helpful to develop investment goals and a strategy on your own, then interview and meet with a financial advisor to confirm that you have no issues or gaps in the map you've charted.

Losing Focus. Don't make the rookie mistake of switching in and out of funds, trying to outpace the market. Decide what no-load index fund matches your needs, and invest, while diversifying your money, accordingly. Otherwise, you waste time and can drive yourself crazy by comparing how your investments measure up to the market (just as you would by comparing yourself to someone else). Instead of getting bogged down on whether your investment is outperforming the market, focus on these four questions: Are you saving in diversified investments? Are you minimizing taxes and costs? Are your investments doing well over time? Are you working toward your goals? If the answer is yes to all four, you're fine.

International Investing. It may be obvious, but avoid investing in areas where the government is unstable or corrupt, or its banking system is composed of kleptomaniacs, because it's too difficult for your dollar to outpace their urge to steal.

Spreads and Fees. When it comes to trading stocks—though you're better off sticking with a no-load index fund—there are discount brokers and full-service brokers. The spread is the difference between the price you buy something for and the price you can sell it for. Another way to think of it is as a markup the broker will charge for handling a transaction. The bigger the spread, the harder it is for you to profit. Although sometimes there's wiggle room in the spread for the broker to shave a bit off for you, don't invest in a stock that has a wide spread without understanding the handicap this places on your chances of making a profit on the particular stock. Fees are another profit killer. Every advisor and transaction comes with a fee, so analyze the true profit earned after fee deductions (and taxes) are taken, accordingly.

AN INVESTMENT STRATEGY FOR THE NEW INVESTOR OR BUSY PROFESSIONAL

For now, stay away from the institutional investor–type investments (i.e., investment vehicles designed for those who are moving money in and out of niche markets quickly) and stick with long-term growth (i.e., holding your money in the market for more than ten years). Presuming your age is 20- or 30-something and you are comfortable with risk, consider an aggressive asset allocation; otherwise, consider a moderate level. Because a stock index fund will match the growth of the stock market without charging high fees for a fund manager, open a no-load stock index fund, such as those offered by Vanguard or Fidelity. Set aside a certain amount a month to deposit—one that won't cause you to lose sleep over whether you're going to lose it. (If you can part with it, 10 percent of your after-tax income arranged as an automatic transfer into the index fund account would be ideal.)

When diversifying your assets, spread the investment over U.S. stock funds, international stock funds, and U.S. bond funds. The purpose of an international allocation is that if the dollar drops dramatically or the U.S. economy overheats, the international investments should balance the domestic investment losses. Don't attempt individual stock picks unless (a) you know the particular industry intimately well and know that you can outpick the analysts, researchers, and other "experts" ("experts" is in quotation marks because, remember, no one can predict the future with 100 percent accuracy), and (b) you are so confident in the company and its product or service that you would own the whole company, if you could. Annually, analyze whether shifting the allocation in the index fund regarding each type of investment over time is necessary—always keeping in mind inflation, interest rates, and the effect of taxes, if any—to achieve strong gains with minimum volatility.

When you've established a good financial footing and educated yourself on investment vehicles, their diversification qualities, and tax consequences, then decide whether the risk is worth it to dive into more complex investment vehicles and strategies. Should you graduate past index funds, when analyzing an investment, make sure you know the business and the product or service it sells and whether the company is competently, efficiently, and honestly managed, and only invest when there's a reasonable expectation for profits, not optimism that the stock will go up. Don't forget to check your client cases to determine whether there are any conflicts in investing that you would have to disclose. Finally, always remember the market is essentially legalized gambling, and you are shouldering the risk. So, above all else, *never* put money in the market if you can't comfortably afford to lose it.

Chapter 8

Taxes

A fool and his money are soon parted. The rest of us have to wait until tax time.

—Anonymous

Taxes will always be here—no matter what the tax protestors argue, nor the political rhetoric spoken at campaign time. Our country also will always call its tax system "voluntary," though the methods of encouraging your compliance may feel like an involuntary servitude (e.g., assessing civil penalties, along with collection via garnishments, seizure, and, in certain circumstances, criminal penalties). This is why what matters in financial decisions is not how much you earn, but how much you will end up with after taxes, because that's really how much money you will get to keep.

THE BASICS

Tax planning is based on minimizing the taxes you pay. An understanding of the W-4 Form, exemptions, and tax brackets is crucial to tax management.

Form W-4

The IRS website (http://www.irs.gov) provides a withholding calculator that can assist in determining the correct amount that should be withheld from your paycheck. In the keywords box, type in "withholding calculator." Use this calculator before completing Form W-4 for your employer instead of committing the mistake of having too much tax withheld from your pay. The general rule is that if you receive a sizable refund, you have had too much withheld. Even if you are too undisciplined to save money, it's better to have an automatic deduction from your paycheck into a savings account than let the IRS have yearlong use of your money interest-free. Similarly, file a new W-4 if you owed over $100 last year when you filed your return, got married or divorced, became a parent, or lost a dependent that you claimed last year on your return.

Know Your Tax Bracket

In the United States, our income is taxed progressively, in layers, with each layer of income being taxed at a higher rate. The layers are brackets, and understanding how the tax bracket rates apply to your income is important to determining how much income you can keep every year. In real-life situations, this means analyzing how much you will really earn if you slave extra hours for a performance bonus, or what the real cost of a mortgage is, after tax, if the interest is deducted, as well as how much of your taxable investment income you can keep. The IRS website offers forms and publications that illustrate the applicable tax brackets for the tax year. Essentially, the higher the annual income, the more tax brackets you'll cross.

> For illustration purposes, assume three tax brackets: 10 percent, 20 percent, and 30 percent. The 10 percent rate applies to income from $1 to $10,000; the 20 percent rate, to $10,001 to $20,000; and the 30 percent, to income above $20,000. Brad earns $65,000. The rate on the first $10,000 would be 10 percent, so he would pay $1,000; at $20,000 the rate is 20 percent, so he would pay $2,000 on the next $10,000 of income earned; and, finally, he would pay 30 percent on the remainder of $45,000 earned, or $13,500. So, he will pay a total of $16,500.

For tax planning purposes, another way to think of this is that the tax rate will tell you the percentage of additional earnings that will go to the IRS. For example, assume Brad, from the accompanying illustration, can earn a $5,000 bonus if he works an extra 500 hours. The federal tax bracket shows his ultimate tax rate is 30 percent. This means 30 percent of that bonus will be paid to the IRS. Brad would also factor in the local and state tax rates, if any. For example, if Brad's state tax rate is 4 percent, then the combined rate is 34 percent (30 percent + 4 percent = 34 percent); thus, 34 percent of the $5,000 bonus would be paid to taxes, so working 500 extra hours would really net Brad $3,300.

Itemizing can also save you money when you have significant, albeit reasonable, unreimbursed business or medical expenses. Should you have no or low mortgage interest, itemizing will likely not apply unless you have incurred unreimbursed business or medical expenses or have made large charitable donations.

Exemptions

Exemptions are deductions from your taxable income. Dependents are exemptions, and the IRS website provides information on how to determine the number of dependents to claim. Exemptions do phase out over certain income levels, however.

PREPARING A RETURN

Even for the most intelligent and educated professional, the thought of preparing a tax return can bring on a headache. However, there are things you can do so the effort won't be so taxing (pun intended), beginning with how you keep track of your finances during the year.

Record Keeping

Maintaining good records is fundamental to preparing a return, whether you prepare the return or hire it out. Detailed, organized receipts, statements, and other documents should be maintained as if you expect to be challenged and have to provide substantiation to establish the deductions and income; merely maintaining a record of your category totals (income, expenses) is insufficient to survive an audit. Unless there's a reason for the IRS to suspect fraud, it's safe to destroy the backup documents corresponding to a particular return after six years (from the date of filing the return) have passed. Notice the word "destroy." Invest in a good paper shredder because that is crucial to preventing identity theft. Maintain storage (electronic or hard copy) for records such as closing documents for the purchase of your home (or its sale) and improvements made to it, retirement accounts, and investment documents.

Hiring Out

Tax professionals have differing degrees of education and experience. Generally, the least educated is an enrolled agent or tax preparer, followed by an accountant and a CPA (certified public accountant), with the most educated being a tax attorney. Enrolled agents, tax preparers, and accountants are retained for the basics, while tax attorneys as well as CPAs are retained for planning and more complex return preparation. As to the forms, the IRS website provides guidance concerning what tax and information returns must be filed, along with instructions, the due dates, and publications that can be ordered for general requirement information.

For an educated professional, the substantive and technical preparation of a Form 1040EZ doesn't require hiring out. If you don't want to put pen to paper, there are software programs that are available to streamline return preparation. Typically, the user is prompted with a series of questions (similar to those that would be asked if you were face-to-face with a preparer). Then the program calculates the amounts owed and produces the finished product based on the information you supplied. Preparing a Form 1040EZ probably isn't worth the monetary investment in software, however, or the fee for a tax preparer.

Likewise, for an educated professional, hiring a tax preparer or accountant may not be worth it if you're filing a Form 1040 for an uneventful financial year. As an educated professional, you are likely capable of reading the IRS form instructions and determining what new laws, if any, apply to your personal situation for purposes of preparing a tax return. It becomes financially worth it to hire out the preparation of your return if you simply find it too much of a time-consuming hassle to prepare it. After all, paying $100 to a licensed tax professional to prepare and file state and federal returns for you when you could be billing your time at $250 an hour is good economic sense. Tax prep fees are also deductible. Either way, the more organized and detailed your records, the better. It saves you time if you do the preparation. Organized record keeping also saves you money if you hire out because a tax professional will likely require less time to prepare the tax return and may charge less, accordingly.

If you're self-employed, quarterly calculations of self-employment income and preparation of forms may prove more time-consuming, and retaining an accountant can be worth it. For returns involving complex investments or business matters, consider retaining a CPA or tax attorney unless you have an accounting or tax background. For example, if you're fortunate to receive the perks enjoyed by CEOs and a handful of other top executives, such as personal use of company aircraft and cars, country club memberships, or housing and relocation costs, know that you may likely find the perk triggering an IRS bill, so it should be included in taxable income. The more complex your finances, the more need to consult an attorney with particular expertise in the substantive area of tax law necessary to help you comply with the applicable laws.

Don't File Early

Don't file your tax return early. Generally, taxpayers who file returns early (well before the "Taxgiving Day" of April 15) have a greater likelihood of being randomly selected for audit.

If You Can't Pay, Still File the Return

When you can't pay the tax shown to be due by the due date for filing the return, you should still file it, or at least file a request for an extension. This is because not filing by the due date can add up to 25 percent to your tax bill in the form of late filing penalties. You are not without options in negotiating payment; however, all of them will require providing the IRS with accurate and detailed financial information. More information can be found on the IRS website concerning the forms that will be required before the IRS will consider discussing a payment plan with you (e.g., Forms 433 and 656). Should you own assets or have savings, expect the IRS to respond that you should use them to pay or apply for a loan and use the proceeds to satisfy the tax owed. Obviously, if the problem in paying occurs because you did not have enough withheld from your paycheck, file a new Form W-4 with your employer so that the error is not repeated on next year's return. As with other matters, negotiating a payment plan with the IRS will likely be more successful (and easier) if you consult a CPA or tax litigator, should you have no previous IRS dispute experience.

Discriminant Function System (DIF)

The Discriminant Function System (DIF) is why much has been written about ways to avoid an audit in return preparation—specifically, ways to out-psych the DIF because the IRS uses it to select returns for audit. Briefly, the DIF is the IRS's scoring system for elements that appear on your return. For example, if you've reported more business-related deductions than the IRS deems normal for someone with your income, your return is going to get some extra points (extra points are not a good thing). If the total score is greater than the IRS guidelines, the computer selects your return for review. Should an agent determine that the return requires an audit, that's when you are contacted.

DEALING WITH THE IRS

According to IRS Publication 1, the IRS's mission is to "provide America's taxpayers top quality service by helping them understand and meet their tax responsibilities and by applying the tax law with integrity and fairness to all." This may be difficult to believe when you receive an ominous envelope containing confusing correspondence spit out by the IRS computer with only a toll-free phone number that, when called, records your discussion after you've spent 45 minutes listening to elevator music while waiting for an IRS employee to answer the line.

Nevertheless, every lawyer has a purpose (at least, that's what the law school enrollment stats suggest), and tax litigators are no exception. If you have no experience dealing with the IRS, give a call to your legal brothers and sisters who routinely negotiate with the IRS before trying to battle the IRS on your own. That being said, because there is inevitably someone who goes it alone, here is some general guidance.

For some IRS inquiries, all that may be required to resolve the issue is a written response providing information or documentation concerning a forgotten Form W-2 or 1099. Other matters may be more complicated. Obviously, the more complex the issues, the more reason to retain a tax professional with the appropriate level of experience and expertise to help you. If you don't want to pay an accountant, attorney, or CPA to help you, at least consider investing in an IRS procedures book that details how to handle audits, dispute assessments, and seek refunds, when appropriate. The IRS bureaucracy has very defined divisions, each with employees responsible for handling certain duties and tasks and only those duties and tasks. More importantly, each level of the IRS has very specific procedures that must be followed and substantive law that will apply to the particular dispute, issue, or subject. One mistake could prove fatal to the success of your case, resulting in your losing the battle before the war you wanted to wage ever begins (hence, the reason tax litigators exist).

Because Dan was a lawyer, he represented himself in an IRS audit, disputing the IRS's assessments of taxes and penalties up to the IRS Appeals Division. After filing suit in court, he learned that he had committed costly IRS procedural errors when the government moved to dismiss Dan's case.

IRS Notices, Demands for Payment

IRS collection actions are serious business. If the IRS has already assessed taxes, penalties, and interest against you, you will receive notices and demands for payment and, eventually, a visit from a not-so-friendly revenue officer assigned to collect the tax liability. The options of an installment agreement or offer-in-compromise may be available to you. Again, the IRS website describes these options in detail. However, if you lack experience with the IRS, consult an attorney who routinely practices with the IRS for your jurisdiction.

STRATEGIES FOR MINIMIZING TAXES

Reducing your adjusted gross income, increasing your deductions such as mortgage interest and charitable contributions, and taking advantage of any credits to which you are entitled are the avenues for minimizing taxes. Highlighted in the following paragraphs are four common approaches to achieving such an accomplishment: tax-deferred investments, tax shelters, real estate, and asset placement.

Tax-Deferred Investments

These are used to postpone paying income taxes. A retirement account is the most typical example. Retirement accounts are the easiest way to grow your money while shrinking your taxes. In fact, the best way to reduce your adjusted gross income is by maxing out your retirement contributions. The higher your combined (local, state, and federal) tax bracket, the better to incorporate investment tax-deferred vehicles into your portfolio. In contrast, the lower the tax bracket, the greater likelihood you can realize better after-tax returns from fully taxable investments.

Tax Shelters

Although many can be based on unsound interpretations of the Internal Revenue Code, some tax shelters are legitimate opportunities to invest in potentially lucrative deals while getting a tax break. Generally speaking, tax shelters are evidence that CPAs, financial planners, and tax lawyers are an entrepreneurial and customer service–oriented bunch. This is because tax shelters will always exist—in some form, name, product, or structure—as long as client demand for them exists. When you have earned enough money to become a potential client, remember this rule: *never* invest in a deal solely for its tax benefits. If you are audited, the IRS will examine the investment from an economic perspective, and that's how you should, too.

A way to determine a tax shelter's actual profit potential is by measuring the potential after-tax return against the after-tax cost. By doing so, you can compare the cost of a tax shelter opportunity with other investment vehicles, such as stocks and bonds, that are acquired with after-tax dollars. Also, factor in how long it will take to get the yield from the after-tax dollars. For example, a three-to-one return ($3 of cash received for each $1 invested) will likely not pass muster with the IRS if it takes several years longer to realize the full profit. The bottom line: if the deal wouldn't be worth the risk for you to invest without the tax benefits, then don't do it—unless you are comfortable with the shelter likely triggering an IRS audit and with the corresponding vacuum on your time and money that an audit can bring.

As a general rule, whenever anyone proposes a "tax-free" investment, be cautious. Often marketed as legitimate investments designed to legally avoid income taxes, "tax-free" vehicles generally are viewed with skepticism by the IRS. The typical scenario occurs where the proposed structure falls within the technical confines of the Internal Revenue Code, thereby making it legal until the U.S. Treasury Department, the IRS, and Congress eventually fix the loophole that is causing the "tax-free" result. Thus, a potential investor's concern becomes twofold: how long before the government catches on, and what are the consequences to an investor when it does? Because there are circumstances in which the IRS will exercise its right to retroactively issue regulations designed to correct a perceived abuse, these concerns become good questions to ask, along with seeking a (second) opinion letter from an independent tax lawyer about the proposed transaction.

Regarding offshore or foreign ventures as a way to hide taxable assets, know that with the treaties and agreements the United States has with so many countries, the IRS will likely track the assets back to you. Never place your assets in offshore investments that lie in countries that have unstable governments. Even if they have no treaties to exchange information with the United States, often the banking and government systems are run by kleptomaniacs who may line their pockets with some of your money for the privilege of their secrecy. Expatriation is another way, albeit extreme, to legally avoid paying taxes; however, satisfying its requirements may come with careful government scrutiny over your activities and assets, too.

Real Estate

Homeowners are allowed to deduct the mortgage interest from their taxable income. Generally, under present law, you can keep up to $250,000 ($500,000 if married) of profit when the home is sold, without paying any taxes on the gain. Not everything associated with home ownership is deductible, however. Association fees and improvements are a common deduction mistake; these expenses are not deductible. However, keep the records for improvements because if you sell, those expenses will be added into your basis. Concerning other real estate investments, be aware that changing tax laws no longer result in depreciation expenses and tax loss deductions as an automatic boost to the rate of return. Specifically, incurred operating or tax losses may not be deductible, so research the tax (and diversification) benefits before investing in real estate.

Asset Placement

This strategy is based on the fact that different investments generate different tax treatments under the Internal Revenue Code. The after-tax, inflation-adjusted return for each investment is analyzed so that assets are placed in an overall portfolio structure that maximizes profits while minimizing taxes. In essence, the diversification and tax advantages (or disadvantages) are analyzed before investing. This strategy becomes especially important when you have graduated to high-yielding, volatile, or complex investment structures generating capital gains and losses.

In sum, there are as many tax planning methods and tax-saving strategies as there are articles and books that you can research to determine which method is best for your situation. Consulting with tax attorneys and CPAs is also recommended, especially for developing advanced planning methods or strategies for high incomes. However, when you become a high-income taxpayer, you'll likely learn that aside from maxing out retirement contributions, there aren't enough legitimate ways to reduce taxes.

Chapter 9

Retirement Planning

Too much of a good thing can be wonderful.

—Mae West

When it comes to money in retirement, having too much of it will be a wonderful thing. Because these days, for many in retirement, the setting sun begins to rise again. Reawakened ambitions, second careers, travel, volunteering, or becoming firebrands for causes about which they're passionate—all of these activities require retirees to have a steady flow of income to fund them. At some point (it is hoped in much later years), health care and physical care options will likely take financial priority. Simply put, how comfortable you are in your retirement years depends on your money and health. Money also will likely dictate where you live and the activities you participate in, so careful retirement planning is important.

THE BASICS: FIGURING OUT HOW MUCH MONEY YOU'LL NEED DURING RETIREMENT

Most Americans will spend an average of 25 to 30 years in retirement, which means you'll need to have 10 to 20 times your salary saved. The financial industry offers gauges for savings rates, as illustrated in the accompanying chart.

Approach the financial industry's gauges with caution. The gauges are based on assumptions that may not apply to you because the gauges assume that (1) retirement occurs at age 67, (2) with 85 percent of an individual's anticipated final salary and Social Security being used as a monthly retirement income flow (3) until age 92. Expenses for long-term care, as well as factors for individual health and lifestyle habits, are excluded. Because retirement is a factual determination, unique to each individual's circumstances, these gauges should not be a substitute for performing your own calculations based on your specific financial, health, and retirement needs. Nonetheless, the gauges from Fidelity and Vanguard estimate retirement savings should be equal to these amounts:

Financial Industry Retirement

Savings Gauges	Age
Begin 6 percent deposit of salary	25
Multiply salary times 1.5	35
Multiply salary times 3	45
Multiply salary times 6	55
Multiply salary times 8	67

Source: Fidelity Investment Retirement study assumes retirement deposits consistent with salary increases of 1.5 percent over general inflation and growth rate averaging 5.5 percent, and consistent 3 percent employer contributions to 401(k) savings; Vanguard Investment Retirement study assumes 401(k) deposits consistently increase for career duration up to 12 percent, plus an employer contribution of 3 percent during the depositor's career.

Consistent saving is difficult for most people because of economic factors impacting law as a profession, but also different practice areas experience booms and busts depending on how the economy fluctuates. For lawyers who experience income fluctuations, an equation of increasing retirement contributions when income increases has a high probability of achieving the necessary savings for retirement needs. For a more specific calculation, many calculators are available on the Internet to help you determine how much money you will need, and they are referenced in Appendix A. Before you use them, however, determine your likely sources of income, your anticipated health care needs, and how you might want to spend your retirement days.

Income Sources

The possible sources of income for most retirees include a 401(k), an IRA, a company pension, savings, investments, and employment. Generally, if you can rely on having at least three of these sources, you should have a comfortable retirement, meaning you can afford the daily living expenses necessary for your lifestyle.

Health Insurance Needs

Health insurance is always a major concern. Once a person reaches age 65, Medicare theoretically kicks in, but you'll need supplemental insurance for what Medicare doesn't cover. Affordable health care is only available for those with no medical conditions, and after 65, it's rare not to have been diagnosed with a physical ailment or medical condition that requires periodic attention. Thus, the bad news is that you must financially prepare for your health insurance premiums to rise as you grow older as well as the prospect of needing long-term care insurance, mentioned in Chapter 6. The good news is that taking care of yourself now can pay off later. Regularly exercising, quitting bad health habits, and maintaining a healthy weight are all things you can do now to try to keep fit and help maintain the lowest premiums possible.

Don't Count on Social Security/Medicare

When calculating the likely income sources during retirement, don't factor in Social Security or Medicare. This is because the oncoming crush of 78 million retiring baby boomers will likely crash the Medicare trust fund by 2019 and the Social Security trust fund by 2041 (unless Congress and the White House find an agreeable cure). So, be prudent and plan as though there will be no Social Security benefits in your future.

Goals

Finally, though they may likely be developing over the next 20 to 30 years, consider your retirement goals. Ponder where and how you want to live, including what you'll do with the luxury of all that free time. Relocating to a sunny climate, owning a second home for a winter retreat, donating time and money to a nonprofit, traveling perpetually from exotic locale to exotic locale—the world can be your oyster if you financially plan right. Don't be among the 39 percent of retirees who responded in a 2007 Fidelity Research Institute survey that they underestimated the amount of their spending and expenses. When you pen your retirement goals, they should match the lifestyle you would like to have 20, 30, or 40 years from now, whenever it is you anticipate retiring.

Inflation

Before discussing retirement investment strategies, an understanding of the effect of inflation on your retirement savings is necessary. Inflation works against your investments. When you calculate the return on an investment, you'll need to consider not just the interest rate you receive but also the real rate of return, which is determined by figuring in the effects of inflation. With the exception of the '80s double-digit inflation rates, the average rate of inflation has been 2 to 4 percent, according to the U.S. Bureau of Labor Statistics. As mentioned in Chapter 7, inflation is an important factor when considering your investment strategy. At first glance, an inflation rate of 4 percent might not be of overwhelming concern, until you consider its application to your purchasing power. For example, 4 percent inflation translates to the value of a dollar decreasing to $0.44. Over 20 years, a $0.41 postage stamp will be $0.87. Applying that rate to a big ticket item, a $23,000 car may command a $50,000 price tag in 20 years. This is important when considering your financial goals because it can reduce the value of your current salary. For example, a $90,000 annual salary will have the buying power of only $86,400 next year if you did not earn a raise to compensate for the 4 percent inflation rate.

TYPES OF RETIREMENT PLANS AND ACCOUNTS

Defined-contribution plans, individual retirement accounts (IRAs), and Keogh plans are the types of retirement vehicles available. (If you work for a corporation, you may have a defined-benefit plan known as a pension. The traditional pension plan will not be discussed because it is becoming a thing of the past as it places much of the retirement savings responsibility on the employer.) These investments are a way to grow your money while saving taxes. With few exceptions, they offer the power of compounding interest while you pay no taxes on your contributions or their earnings until you withdraw the money after age 59½. (Withdraw before that age, and the IRS will impose ordinary income tax and an early withdrawal penalty.) By age 70½, you have to start withdrawals or face a penalty of 50 percent of the minimum distribution amount.

Defined-Contribution Plans

Most employers offer some form of a defined-contribution plan. Your contributions (and those of your employer, if applicable) are kept in an individual account in your name. The advantage of this plan is that you can decide how your money will be invested. The plan will set the terms of how frequently you can change the allocation on your investment choices. If you change jobs, you can take the money with you and roll it over to another retirement vehicle. The most common plans include a 401(k) (private employers), a 403(b) (nonprofits, tax-exempt employers), and a 457 (government, nonprofit employers). Others are money purchase plans, profit-sharing plans, thrift or savings plans (TSAs), and savings incentive match plans (SIMPLEs).

401(k): An employer-sponsored retirement plan whereby participating employees receive a tax break for saving for their retirement. Contributions are deducted from your paycheck, before your taxes are calculated. You don't pay tax on the earnings until you withdraw them—presumably at retirement—at which point, your investment grows faster because your untaxed earnings benefit from compounding. Some employers may match a percentage of your contributions (e.g., $0.50–$1 to every $1 you deposit), though the law applies a cap on the matching amount. The employer match is usually subject to vesting after you've been there a few years. Otherwise, you're always 100 percent vested in your contributions. Contribute to the 401(k); don't walk away from free money. Limits on the contribution are adjusted by the IRS every year. Other limits for lower versus highly compensated employees may also apply unless your employer has adopted a safe-harbor provision for all eligible employees.

403(b), 457: These plans operate much like a 401(k), except that in a 457 plan, the account is funded solely by the employee's contributions. No employer matching contributions are permitted.

Individual Retirement Accounts (IRAs)

Several variations of IRAs are offered by financial institutions, mutual funds, or brokers. As with a 401(k), the IRS sets the contribution limits annually. If you do not have access to an employer-sponsored plan, open one of the following types of IRAs. Otherwise, max out your contribution to the employer plan first. Nondeductible contributions may still be made, and the earnings on those contributions are exempt from tax until the money is withdrawn. For any nondeductible contributions made (except for a Roth), keep records so you won't be taxed again when you withdraw. Withdrawing nondeductible funds before age 59½ will cause the IRS to treat the withdrawal as a proportionate blend of both the nondeductible and deductible contributions, so a penalty in some proportion may apply.

Traditional IRA: Whether contributions to an IRA are tax deductible depends on your income and whether you are participating in a qualified retirement plan at work. (If your contributions are not tax deductible, then you should consider a Roth, discussed next.) Presuming your income isn't greater than the annual limit set by the IRS, if you (and your spouse) do not participate in any employer-provided retirement plan, you can deduct the contributions made to the IRA. As with the 401(k), the money grows tax-deferred until you withdraw funds at retirement when they are taxed at your regular income tax rate. You have up to and including April 15 to make a contribution for the previous tax year; just make certain you make contributions before you file your income tax return because the IRS will verify the contribution date.

Roth IRA: Contributions to a Roth are not deductible, but the earnings are never taxed. Unlike the traditional IRA where you're required to withdraw a minimum amount each year once you turn 70½, a Roth has no such requirement. The IRS does place limits on the amount you can contribute based on your income, however. You should delay distributions from Roth IRAs for as long as possible because the income that builds up is tax-free.

Simple IRAs, SEPs: A Savings Incentive Match Plan for Employees (SIMPLE) IRA is for businesses with no other retirement plans and with fewer than 100 employees. Your contributions and earnings are tax-deferred, and the IRS requires the employer to match contributions, with certain limitations on the matching amount. Simplified Employee Pension (SEP) IRAs are similar to SIMPLEs except only the employer can contribute. The disadvantage is that you have no control over how much money goes into your plan. If you are participating in either a SEP or SIMPLE, you can still invest in a traditional or Roth IRA, however.

Keogh Plans

These plans are for people who have self-employment income. Though the IRS no longer uses the term "Keogh," many still refer to profit-sharing and money purchase plans as "Keoghs." In a money purchase plan, the same contribution each year is required even if you haven't made any profits. The contribution amount is limited by the IRS. Likewise, with profit-sharing plans, the contributions are limited, but the amount can change each year.

Summary Account Benefits for Solo/Small-Firm Practitioners Amounts and Contribution Deadline for 2013 Is April 15, 2014

SEP IRA	SIMPLE IRA	401(K) SAFE HARBOR	DEFINED BENEFIT PLAN
• No employees • No reporting • Easy to start • IRS sets maximum employer contribution • Best used by firm needing cash-flow flexibility	• With employees • IRS sets owner contribution every year • Employees get dollar-for-dollar employer match up to 3 percent of employee salary • Discretionary maximum contribution for owner allowing flexibility to cash-flow uncertainties • Best used by low-income earner	• With employees • Same as SIMPLE IRA but permits higher owner contributions. IRS sets maximum contribution limit annually. • Higher administrative cost than SIMPLE • Lower cost than defined plan • Best used by firm whose earnings vary year-to-year	• With employees • Professional help needed for compliance and IRS reporting requirements • Best used by high-income earner who may need to catch up on savings

INHERITED IRA

Estate planning and tax attorneys are aware that an inherited IRA can be used as a vehicle for transferring wealth to one's heirs. However, for purposes of retirement planning and estate planning, it must be mentioned that the 2014 U.S. Supreme Court's ruling in *Clark v. Rameker* no longer makes assets held in an inherited IRA account protected from creditors in the event of bankruptcy filing. This is important for estate planning purposes as *Clark v. Rameker* says that an inherited individual retirement account (IRA) does not qualify as retirement funds for the purposes of bankruptcy exemption. Because the heir to the fund (other than the spouse) is not permitted to make contributions to the account, the Supreme Court held the accounts do not fall under the definition of a retirement fund.

RULES OF RETIREMENT INVESTING

Follow the rules summarized here when investing for retirement.

Start Early. You'll realize the maximum appreciation in your investments and recoup a loss should there be any disappointing investments. The reason? Compound interest over a long savings horizon.

> Assume Kelly starts saving $200 at age 25, averaging 6 percent compounded annually. By age 60, the estimated accumulated amount would be $566,980.16 versus starting at age 30, which accumulates $402,248.05.

Save 10 Percent. Historically, the financial industry has long recommended that you should save at least 10 percent of your annual adjusted gross income toward retirement, regardless of whether the contributions are taxable. Consistent saving every year is the best way to achieve a comfortable retirement nest egg. If that's a difficult savings rate—as it is for many who graduated with significant student debt—then look for ways to save even 1, 2, or 3 percent of your paycheck to allocate toward retirement savings. Even if you can only afford $10 per month, do it now! Truly, even 1 percent makes a difference to further your retirement savings goals. To see how that 1 percent affects your paycheck, go to http://www.mutualfundstore.com/find-money-investing-calculator or http://www.aarp.org/work/retirement-planning/contributions_paycheck_calculator/?intcmp=AE-BLIL-DOTORG.

Increase Savings with Increased Earnings. Consistent savers contributing 10 to 15 percent of their annual income have a high probability of achieving the industry recommendation of having 75 to 85 percent of preretirement income for their retirement. However, being a lawyer means earnings can be subject to fluctuations. Depending on the economy or client development, private practitioners, especially those who work contingency cases, can have annual income fluctuations. Income fluctuations often do not allow for consistent savings practices for retirement. For folks who are late retirement saving starters or inconsistent savers due to earnings fluctuations, research from Dimensional Fund Advisors (DFA) based in Austin, Texas, which studied various scenarios for investors who experience earnings fluctuations, offers retirement hope. After simulating the effect of retirement investment strategies among differing income levels, savings rates, and varying spending needs, DFA's researchers suggest that if investors who are unable to save consistently increase their contributions to retirement savings when their earnings increase and engage in proper diversification and asset allocation, they may have a likelihood of achieving a good preretirement income replacement rate.

With Youth Comes Agility; Be Aggressive. The longer you have to invest, the more that time will make up for any short-term losses. The corollary to this is that the younger you are, the more aggressive the investment can be. If you don't plan on retiring within the next 30 years, the bulk of your retirement account should be in stocks or stock index mutual funds because you have several decades before you'll need the money. (Contrast: if you were saving to buy a home in a few years, the down payment money would be better put in a conservative investment, such as a certificate of deposit.)

Portfolio Allocation. Be conscious of your overall portfolio asset allocation. Analyze the diversification and tax consequences of your retirement investments alone, but also as the retirement investments fit in with your overall portfolio asset allocation. Retirement time horizon and risk tolerance determine an investor's diversification and asset allocations.

Stock Allocations. The general rule is the longer the investment horizon, the more risk that can be tolerated. This means the assets in your retirement account have the longest horizon in comparison to other assets in your portfolio because it will be decades before you withdraw them. Yet, diversification is just as important to retirement funds as to your overall portfolio. So, don't invest everything in one stock. For overall portfolio asset allocation purposes, be aware that capital losses realized inside a retirement plan are not deductible. Proper diversification is having your money in stocks in thousands of different companies, across several different sectors and different countries, along with bonds and other assets.

Savings rate, diversification, and asset allocation: the investment trifecta for a comfortable retirement.

Rebalancing means to adjust your portfolio's asset exposures according to long-term asset allocation targets. Rebalancing is a way for investors to maintain their original asset allocation—despite the ups and downs of the markets—by adding or selling stocks and bonds in their portfolios. The often-asked question is, how often should an investor rebalance a portfolio? First, understand that the answer involves assessing the tax consequences and transaction fees incurred for rebalancing. Second, advice differs in the financial industry between two schools of thought. Some advisors suggest to not follow a calendar timetable but, rather, rebalance when the market experiences dives or peaks that significantly impact your original allocations. These advisors may possess software programs that allow ease in rebalancing; again, tax considerations must be factored in, along with transaction fees, for rebalancing. The second school of thought is the traditional financial industry wisdom, which says that it has been sufficient for an investor to review his or her portfolio and rebalance once or twice a year. A commonly used gauge for rebalancing is when your original asset allocation is 10 percentage points or more off base. To tailor savings objectives with rebalancing purposes, there are two online tools to consider for help in assessing whether an asset allocation is right for your retirement needs: bankrate.com's calculator at http://www.bankrate.com/calculators/retirement/asset-allocation.aspx and cnn.com's calculator at http:// money.cnn.com/tools/assetallocwizard/assetallocwizard.html.

"Annual rebalancing is likely to be preferred when taxes or substantial time/costs are involved."
Vanguard Group's 2010 study

Liquidity Allocation. Don't put all your cash in the IRA. Keep some outside the plan for emergency due to the early withdrawal ordinary income tax and penalty.

Bond Allocations. Tax-deferred, compounded earnings are the benefits of placing certain bonds in your retirement account. High-yielding bonds, in general, produce current income each year. Don't place tax-free bonds (e.g., municipal bonds, Series EE bonds) that are sold by federal, state, or local governments in retirement accounts. By putting these tax-favored instruments in a tax-deferred vehicle, the income earned becomes taxable when you withdraw money from your retirement plan, thereby effectively converting a tax-free investment into a low-earning, taxable one. (Series EE bonds are not subject to state income tax, but are taxed at the federal level, usually only when you redeem them.)

Juggling Debt. Being in debt isn't permission to blow off retirement investing. It does mean that once the credit cards are paid off, you must max out your retirement contributions and play catch-up by making (nondeductible) IRA contributions.

Emergencies. Maintain an emergency fund, as discussed elsewhere in this text. Only as a last option, consider withdrawing from your IRA if you're certain to have enough cash to replenish the withdrawal by opening another IRA within 60 days. You can do this only once during a 12-month period.

AGE-APPROPRIATE RETIREMENT INVESTMENT STRATEGIES

Invest in a no-load stock index fund. On average, a well-chosen stock index fund compounding under the retirement canopy should outperform an investment in bonds or life insurance. If your investment horizon is at least 30 years off, you can financially handle an allocation of 80 to 90 percent of your retirement money to a broad-based U.S. stock index fund with the remaining 10 to 20 percent to an international fund. As discussed in Chapter 7, if you don't want to (or can't) take the time to actively manage your retirement account, the index fund approach gives you a good financial base. If you will be manually adjusting your asset allocation (versus using a fund such as Vanguard or Fidelity that can offer automatic adjustments of the asset allocations for you as you age), select your asset allocations making certain that your U.S. stock funds have a mix of large cap, medium cap, and small cap stocks, as well as a mix of value stocks and growth stocks. The following age-dependent strategies are also worth considering.

20-Somethings: Sign up for your employer's plan and save enough for the matching contribution, if available. If no employer retirement plan is available, enroll in a Roth IRA and deposit the annual maximum amount. If you can't save the maximum, save what you can. For asset allocation, consider the chart shown earlier in this chapter for manual allocations. Otherwise, buy one fund, such as those offered by Fidelity, Vanguard, or T. Rowe Price, that can make the age-appropriate allocation automatically for you.

30-Somethings: Pump up the retirement investments. When you receive a bonus or raise, put as much as you can afford in retirement savings. (If a lump-sum deposit of your bonus is too austere, consider a gradual monthly increase.) Want to retire early or reduce taxes? If you've already maxed your contribution to the work plan, open an IRA, preferably a Roth. Don't let one stock dominate your retirement savings; spread the stock allocation over several different players, as illustrated in the preceding chart. This is true even if you've been working at a company in which you've invested your retirement savings; no one stock should ever exceed more than 10 percent of your portfolio. Don't let your financial health be so dependent on a single company's health. Finally, if you're about to vest (i.e., keep more of your employer's contributions), financially, it is usually best to wait to change jobs.

40-Somethings: If you've consistently maxed out retirement contributions for the past 10 to 15 years, you should be on track and need only adjust the allocation in accordance with the previous chart and consider opening an IRA. Conversely, if you've neglected your savings, you must make the sacrifices necessary to max out on contributions to your employer plan *now* and open an IRA for catch-up savings. A Roth IRA has contribution limits set annually, but it is another vehicle for maximizing retirement savings. Unconvinced that you need another retirement vehicle? If you're considering saving for a child's college education instead of your retirement, consider this: there are no scholarships for retirement. So, don't make yourself one of the 46 percent of retirees, mentioned earlier in a study, who has to return to work.

Regardless of age, diversify your assets, especially those within the stock index fund you choose for your retirement dollars. Automatic deductions to the retirement account are always the most disciplined way to save. Finally, whatever your age, the sooner you starting saving, the better. Reaching your retirements goals rests entirely on your shoulders. Don't put off saving, because whatever your retirement goals turn out to be, there is one certainty: retirement will cost money.

Chapter 10

Life Events

A pessimist is one who makes difficulties of his opportunities and an optimist is one who makes opportunities of his difficulties.

—Harry Truman

The adage that life is what happens while we're making plans should encourage you toward financial preparedness. No one can predict what the future will bring, but having your finances ready can make life's events (both good and bad) less tolling on your bank account and, in some circumstances, your emotional state when they occur.

JOB LOSS

Terminations and Layoffs: Few people who've been in this situation started the job feeling their position was insecure. Planning for a potential job loss focuses on health and retirement issues. For your financial health, maintain the emergency fund, discussed in Chapters 1 and 2, and learn what happens to your benefits. Specifically, termination for cause results in COBRA ineligibility. As discussed in Chapter 6, without health insurance, an accident or illness could financially break you. Health insurance becomes an expense for which you'll have to save, and increase your emergency savings fund, accordingly. Retirement plans present other choices: rollover the funds to an IRA, or possibly to your future new employer's plan or, depending on the balance in your account, keep it in the former employer's plan. Finally, careerwise, keep your résumé updated with references ready.

When a *Fortune* 500 corporation slashed its outside counsel roster from 400 to 23 law firms, Marc's firm was not one of the lucky 23. When the work dried up, the firm laid him off, even though he was a capable third-year associate. Because his former colleagues' résumés were saturating the market, his job search to land a comparable salary lasted for months.

JOB CHANGE

On average, attorneys will likely change jobs at least twice during their career—sometimes for better pay or experience, other times because they have no choice for employment. Health concerns dictate that you review the benefits you'll have at the new job versus those needed for purposes of whether COBRA is applicable. Retirement options are the same as those discussed in the preceding "Job Loss" section; however, vesting issues may take the forefront. If you are about to vest in the employer's retirement plan (meaning own more of the employer's contributions), hold off on the job change. Bouncing from job to job before vesting can significantly set you back in saving for your retirement needs.

I Hate My Job! For readers new to the working world, this may be a shocking concept, but there may come a day when the job or career path you have chosen is not everything that you hoped it would be. Worse, despite your best efforts to make your working environment challenging and enjoyable, the only thing keeping you there is the paycheck. If you aren't debt-free and armed with an emergency savings fund, the employer's paycheck dangling in front of you becomes the stick instead of the carrot. Being debt-free with an emergency savings fund will give you the greatest luxury of all: the freedom to say "I'm not doing this anymore." You can quit, take a break, or switch to another occupation altogether, without sacrificing food and shelter.

BURNOUT

Not to dampen your enthusiasm, but there's a reason stress management books are best sellers among lawyers. The legal world can present an environment that nurtures burnout. Against the backdrop of enormous time pressures, the higher your salary, the more pressure on productivity and hours, which can exacerbate the very quality-of-life issues that can make even the most ambitious and talented people unhappy. Leaving the law is a path some attorneys may follow. To ensure that building wealth remains possible, paying off debt, maintaining an emergency fund, and consistently maxing out retirement contributions should be accomplished before the legal career ends. That's not to say that if burnout happens to you, another lucrative career isn't possible. There are many occupations where a law degree and background are helpful. Still, without an emergency fund established, you'll rapidly incur consumer debt, forcing you into a job you'll likely hate.

SABBATICAL

Some firms sponsor paid sabbaticals, although before you can be eligible to participate you have to be anointed partner and then toil for at least seven more years. (Sort of like dangling the carrot on the stick if you're already an overworked associate or new partner.) If you've been slaving in a job that doesn't offer such a future reward, the idea of a self-imposed sabbatical may be appealing.

> Quitting a lucrative associate's job at a high-powered firm, Bob, a skilled New York lawyer, opted for a self-imposed two-month sabbatical on the high seas. Fulfilling a lifelong dream of learning to sail a 54-foot sailboat offered him the advantage of not only mastering a new skill but also gaining a fresh perspective on teamwork, leadership, and the practice of law. Returning recharged and physically fit (and tan), he accepted another high-paying job with an equally high-profile Wall Street firm.

Should the traditional partnership track be your personal holy grail, voluntarily quitting your job or seeking a temporary leave of absence will postpone it. However, when you're good at what you do, you normally don't have to boast about it—people know it. If you're the type of person who works so that you're not just better than the competition but are known as the only person who can do what you do, your career may not be damaged by taking a self-imposed sabbatical for a month or two. In contrast, the same might not be true about your financial health unless you adequately prepare. Save enough to cover your annual retirement contribution and daily living expenses (so you don't charge up the credit cards) and to sustain your emergency fund before you embark on a sabbatical to volunteer for Greenpeace, stump for a political campaign, explore the world, or fulfill a lifelong dream. How to approach this with a current employer? Firms that have joined the sabbatical trend find that partner sabbaticals can make for a more productive (and loyal) partner; the same should be true for associates. Obviously, this argument is much more persuasive when it isn't spoken from the mouth of a first-year associate, so if you're still early in your career, consider why you want the sabbatical. If you're unhappy at work, it may be that you really want a permanent sabbatical from the law, or simply from your employer; therefore, taking a self-imposed temporary sabbatical will only be a Band-Aid, not a cure, for the real problem.

RELATIONSHIPS AND FINANCES

Financial preparedness extends to relationships. Certain relationships come with more financial responsibilities than others, and keeping your financial house in order becomes even more important when others are financially dependent on you.

Skeptical? Jeffrey Dew, an assistant professor in the Department of Family, Consumer, and Human Development at Utah State University, studies money, debt, and savings and their impact on couples and families. He shared his insights from findings gained by studies he wrote during his research.

Q. What are important takeaways from the research and studies on the topic of how debt, savings, and money may affect couples?

A. The idea that debt might affect your "relationship bottom line" is important. This idea that what we do financially might impact our relationships—and not just our wallets—is really important for married couples to keep in mind. They are in a financial relationship and an emotional relationship and these two things influence each other.

These findings also point to the reality that money underlies every relationship. We all need money. Even those who say that they are not motivated by money need it to pay for shelter, food, and other basic necessities. Everyone makes purchases on a near-daily basis.

I think another important "take home message" is that fighting about money is really a strong predictor of divorce. In one of my studies we measured the frequency of five common types of arguments that couples had—money, chores, sex, in-laws, and spending time together. We then examined whether the couples had gotten divorced five years after they were first measured. For the husbands, money was the only argument type to predict divorce. For wives, arguments about money and sex both predicted divorce, but arguments about money were the strongest predictors. The findings from our research showed that couples who reported disagreeing about money and finances once a week were 30 percent more likely to divorce compared to couples who reported disagreeing about money and finances a few times a month. We think that the money arguments predicted divorce because they were strongly linked with feelings of unfairness about money in the relationship, with dissatisfaction in the relationship, and with worse conflict tactics in the marriage (e.g., couples with more money arguments would use shouting more during their arguments and calm discussions less).

One final interesting point from my studies is that sometimes when spouses fight about money, they really aren't fighting about the money. They're really fighting about deeper relationship issues like trust, autonomy, or power. Money might be just the smokescreen, if you will, that masks what they are really fighting about. The conflicts might focus on "who bought what," but underlying those arguments about money may be issues of trust, power, or even relationship insecurities.

Q. What are the most common debts that you've seen cause conflicts in relationships?

A. Consumer debt (e.g., credit card debt or an installment loan from your local furniture store) is associated with more conflicts and problems than a home mortgage. Consumer debt is a unique type of debt because it is so readily available, the interest rates are typically higher than other types of debt, and consumers have the option of paying very low minimum payments. It's really easy to let consumer debt get out of hand. Couples with increased consumer debt tend to fight more because they are more stressed over money and how to pay their bills. One of my studies even showed that consumer debt was associated with a greater likelihood of divorce, which wasn't the case for mortgage debt or student debt.

On the flip side, my findings show that when a couple has liquid savings (e.g., a savings account), it permits them to take the financial pressure off—or at least some of the financial pressure—and to focus on each other and the relationship rather than their financial problems. Having savings set aside seems to allow individuals and couples to have some breathing room. They are less stressed. They fight less about money. They are also less likely to divorce. In one of my studies, savings was even associated with wives', but not husbands', feelings of marital happiness.

Q. Does the level of wealth a couple or individual has make a difference in how often couples argue or are in conflict about money?

A. My studies suggest that it's not about how much money you make, it's about what you do with what you make, and whether your spouse also wants to do that. Higher-income couples fight about money, too, and they get divorced because of it just like lower-income couples. Everyone comes into a relationship with his or her own ideas about money—what money is, whether or how you save it, or spend it. These are topics that everyone, regardless of income, may experience conflict with in their relationships.

Of course, lower-income couples may have more worry and stress about money, which may in turn hurt the relationship. The more [a couple] or one spouse is worrying about finances, the harder time your relationship may have because of the stress that comes with worrying about paying your bills. From my own experience when I was simultaneously a husband, father, and graduate student I can say that it can be hard to sustain a positive marriage relationship when you are worried about whether you have enough food to last you until your next paycheck.

Debt can also play a role as I mentioned before. Oftentimes a couple that lives within their means will be happier than another couple who is accumulating debt but are earning a higher income. Consumer debt, at any level of income, seems to be related to individual stress and relationship difficulties.

Q. Do you have any suggestions for anyone who has never thought about what money "is"?

A. I'd suggest that you think about what your views about money are. What do you think is the best way to use money? What types of intangibles do you find yourself buying with money? For example, do you use money to purchase "status" or "security"? Also, what "money rules" did you learn in your family as you grew up? For example, when we would go to fill up the tank with gas, my dad would often tell us how expensive convenience store soda was relative to the soda you buy at the grocery store. To this day I still have a subconscious aversion to buy[ing] things in a convenience store. So really think about the motives behind your own personal financial behaviors. Then talk about that with your spouse or partner. It will help you understand each other better.

All of us are different. So, it's easy to understand that individual spouses would have different meanings for money. Most couples, when they first meet each other, aren't talking about their finances, or their financial future, or checking to see whether they are financially compatible with each other. When you first start a relationship, you're likely looking at whether you're emotionally compatible. Oftentimes, couples might just assume their compatible everywhere else because they are in love and have emotional compatibility. But, we all grow up in different families, and [because of] what you experience growing up when it comes to money and how your family handles it, you come to an understanding of what money is "best" used for. This is why differences of opinion exist among spouses, and conflict over money can arise. For example, you can have one spouse think money is for fun and interesting experiences, while the other associates money as being used as status, or gaining peace of mind and economic security. These underlying meanings about money make it important for couples to recognize it, talk about it, and work together to set jointly held financial goals. You can't avoid all conflicts over money, but you can minimize conflicts.

Q. Do you have any suggestions for couples to follow to travel down the path of bliss as it relates to money and debt?

A. Just because a couple is in a higher income bracket doesn't correlate to being happier in their relationship or their finances. Communication and fairness about money seems to correlate most strongly with couples reporting that they feel happy in their relationship. In other words, couples may fight less about money because they have already talked and listened to each other about what each does with it.

Listening to each other is so important. Spouses need to feel that their needs and feelings were heard by the other spouse when it comes to finances. Both spouses need to feel that the way money is being handled in the relationship is fair. Feelings of financial unfairness in the marriage was one of the things that linked financial arguments and divorce in one of my studies.

I also can't overstate the importance of couples sitting down and formulating some jointly held financial goals. Both spouses need to agree on these goals and both agree to work toward them. When couples work toward jointly held goals—including financial goals—it creates a real spirit of companionship and unity. The reason is that they are in agreement about what they are doing—whether it's paying off debt, or saving—they've listened to each other and now they are working together.

Of course, you have to recognize that discussing the topic of finances itself could bring about tension. So couples may want to do things to make the conversation fun or more relaxed by listening to music, or having a treat. That can calm things down so that they can have a relaxed, non-adversarial discussion about money.

> The importance of couples getting in sync over finances becomes even more apparent when considering a survey released by TD Ameritrade Inc. and LearnVest in 2013 of couples married or living together between the ages of 18 and 82. The survey revealed:
>
> 40 percent of respondents did not completely trust their partner to manage their combined finances;
>
> 38 percent were only somewhat, slightly, or not at all aware of their significant other's debts;
>
> 21 percent sometimes hid their spending from their significant other.

Moving In Together

Next to someone appearing desperate or too needy, talking about how to spend money can be a romantic mood killer. Nevertheless, if you're serious about a long-term relationship with someone, the money discussion is crucial to both emotional and financial happiness. The agenda for the money discussion does not include bragging about how fat your paycheck is (or whining about how slim). Rather, take the Spender Quiz in Appendix B and let the discussion unfold. Inevitably, couples who are unable to honestly discuss financial issues and reach moderate compromises (when they differ) are in for either a tumultuous relationship, bankruptcy, or both. So, if you're serious about sharing your life with someone, let the romance temporarily wane for an hour and discuss your respective attitudes toward money and how it is spent and saved.

Ironically, few cohabiting lawyers actually have a cohabitation agreement for themselves—though lawyers make a mint off people who move in together without a cohabitation agreement. If you're one of these cohabiting people, though you may rationalize that, as a lawyer, you can argue your way out of anything, put it off no more (especially if you have a psychologically sound friend in your trusted circle who is telling you that your beloved is not for you). Without a cohabitation agreement, you're sabotaging all the hard work you've done in creating a financial plan. Think of it in billable time: one hour at your computer drafting up contractual terms versus months consumed by fighting over who gets the love nest and Fido, should domestic bliss end.

Finally, consider whether a health care proxy or health care power of attorney is needed. (This allows someone to make your medical decisions for you when you can't do so.) This is important for couples living together, especially same-sex couples in those states where such relationships are not legally recognized, because some hospitals or medical facilities will not automatically accord visitation privileges to individuals that state law would consider nonrelatives in emergencies. Registered domestic partners or same-sex spouses are legally recognized family members in states recognizing those relationship statuses. Consequently, access to each other in a hospital or other medical facility's restricted-access medical unit (e.g., ICU) would be allowed to the extent any other legally related family member would be allowed by the hospital or medical facility in those states recognizing those relationships. If you are in a state that has not yet enacted legislation recognizing your relationship, a HIPAA Authorization Health Care

Power of Attorney requires a medical provider to allow each partner access to the other in any state. This document spells out who can visit you, who can set the visitation list, and who the patient is designating as family. Note that though a HIPAA Authorization Health Care Power of Attorney can give your significant other authority to make decisions on your behalf, a separate document usually has to be drafted that authorizes your significant other to see and get copies of your medical records under the regulations for HIPAA (the Health Insurance Portability and Accountability Act), a necessity for filing insurance claims, obtaining second opinions, and making informed decisions.

Getting Hitched

Whether you're having a wedding or a commitment ceremony, before you say "I do," discuss finances. Money—controlling it, hiding it, spending it, saving it—is a primary reason couples divorce. Even if you don't view divorce as a likelihood, money issues can turn an otherwise happy union into a battleground. If you're contemplating tying the knot, save yourselves the arguments, heartaches, and worries by discussing your goals and agreeing on a plan for how your combined finances will be earned, saved, and spent. Should you find yourself in the unfortunate situation where your soon-to-be is carrying a horrendous debt load and a credit rating to match, it is financially wise to consider a long engagement until they are improved. Even though it may be emotionally difficult to postpone the wedding bells, consider that a couple beginning a union with a struggling inability to keep creditors at bay is statistically likely to hear the rustling of divorce papers in their future.

For same-sex couples, the U.S. Supreme Court found Section 3 of the Defense of Marriage Act (DOMA) to be unconstitutional in *United States v. Windsor*, 133 S. Ct. 2675 (2013), affording recognition of same-sex marriages for federal purposes. The U.S. Justice Department also issued a formal policy memorandum instructing employees that it is the Justice Department's policy "to recognize lawful same-sex marriages as broadly as possible" and "treat all individuals equally regardless of sexual orientation." (The memorandum can be found online at http://www.justice.gov/iso/opa/resources/9201421014257314255.pdf.)

With the repeal of DOMA, same-sex married couples have access to more than 1,100 federal benefits and protections. For instance, IRS Notice 2014-01 provides guidance on the application of rules concerning health savings accounts (HSAs) and flexible spending accounts (FSAs) to same-sex couples after the Supreme Court's *United States v. Windsor* decision finding the Defense of Marriage Act to be unconstitutional. The question-and-answer section of the notice sets forth that for a cafeteria plan where a participant who was married to a same-sex spouse as of June 26, 2013, the date of the *Windsor* decision, the IRS will treat such participant as if he or she experienced a change in legal marital status. Consequently, a cafeteria plan can allow a taxpayer to revoke an existing election and make a new election in a manner consistent with the change in legal marital status. For purposes of election changes due to the *Windsor* decision, election made with respect to a same-sex spouse (and/or the spouse's dependents) must satisfy the requirements of the regulations concerning election changes generally, including the consistency rule under Treas. Reg. 1.125-4(c)(3). Likewise, a cafeteria plan may permit a participant's FSA, including a health, dependent care, or adoption assistance FSA, to reimburse covered expenses of the participant's same-sex spouse or the same-sex spouse's dependent that were incurred during a period beginning on a date that is no earlier than (a) the beginning of the cafeteria plan year that includes the date of the *Windsor* decision or (b) the date of marriage, if later. Consequently, the same-sex spouse may be treated as covered by the FSA (even if the participant had initially elected coverage under a self-only FSA) during that period.

The IRS issued Revenue Ruling 2013-17 providing that a couple is treated as "legally married" if (1) they are married and reside in a state that allows same-sex marriages or (2) they are married in a state that allows same-sex marriages (even if they should later reside in a state that prohibits same-sex marriages). However, individual states continue to be in transition, some legally recognizing same-sex relationships, others not doing so, with challenges pending. Challenges to same-sex marriage bans have been successful, with courts striking down bans, via lawsuits brought by same-sex couples seeking to force their particular state of residence to recognize their out-of-state marriages. In the interim, the U.S. Department of Justice policy memorandum of 2014 provides that the federal government recognizes same-sex marriage to the fullest extent possible under the law, even in states that do not allow it. Certain limitations apply in that the policy only applies where the U.S. government has jurisdiction.

For all couples contemplating marriage, the potential for the "marriage penalty" to impact their taxes exists. Indeed, getting married normally increases a couple's tax bill, unless they structure it so that one of the soon-to-be spouses isn't generating income. Like all tax provisions, the marriage penalty is subject to legislative changes.

The Tax Policy Center has a calculator to determine whether the marriage penalty applies to you at http://taxpolicycenter.org/taxfacts/marriagepenaltycalculator.cfm.

A second personal exemption deduction becomes available to the working spouse, and both spouses can make annual IRA contributions, potentially decreasing a married couple's total adjusted gross income. On the other hand, if both of you will be working, review each employer's health coverage and determine which health plan offers better benefits. Do the same review with retirement accounts. Ultimately, merge your record keeping and bill paying systems together into one concise, yet thorough, method.

Remember to:

____Update financial records/accounts to reflect ownership changes.
____Consolidate accounts where it makes financial sense.
____Make sure deeds, titles, etc., are correctly worded for ownership.
____Verify that processing of all beneficiary forms is done correctly.

Finally, a prenuptial agreement becomes a must-have wedding gift when you live in a community property state or may inherit valuable (or sentimental) assets (or the psychologically balanced person in your trusted circle is advising you to run). Even if your betrothed has promised to never take something you hold near and dear, a person's memory can fade after living in luxury, especially when the prospect of it ending is near—put it in writing.

Getting or Giving the Boot

Just like investing in the wrong stock, when you invest in a relationship with the wrong person, it often doesn't pay off. However, when JLo recorded "Love Don't Cost a Thing," it must have been before she divorced because then the primary question will be "How much is it gonna cost me?" After the emotional trauma and child or pet custody issues, the bottom line is money. This book is not advocating that committed couples include divorce in their financial plan. Rather, this section is for those who are already contemplating it, are going through it, or have already done it. Despite having a good divorce lawyer to advise concerning the custodial and property issues, most divorced couples seldom come out financially ahead when the ink is dry on the order of dissolution. To ensure that any financial setback is only temporary, during or after a divorce, consult a licensed financial advisor who is certified in divorce planning aftermath, if only to confirm that your strategy for getting back on financial track and building wealth is a good practice.

BECOMING A CAREGIVER

Many professionals may find themselves sidelined, at some point, to handle family responsibilities. Whether caring for an elderly parent or having a child, becoming a caregiver can sap your finances if you haven't financially prepared for it. Some trendsetting employers offer flexible work schedules and telecommuting that allow you to fulfill both home and work responsibilities. If you don't have that option, preparing a budget that allows you to hire help or quit working will keep your promising financial future intact. On average, it can take up to five years for every one year you are not working to recapture lost benefits and savings and to get up to speed on the pay scale when you opt back in to the workforce. Therefore, protect your retirement by continuing to max out your annual contributions.

Concerning your aging parents, be proactive and have a talk about planning for their long-term care needs. Most children also end up handling their parents' estate when they die. Yes, the inevitable is a sensitive subject, but there's no need to become the Addams Family. View the situation as you would any other client problem that you've been asked to analyze. You're simply troubleshooting and developing a plan for contingencies. Gently broach the topic with your parents, have the talk, make a plan, and, it is hoped, the subject will not be reopened for a very long time. Still apprehensive? Estate attorneys earn thousands assisting beneficiaries and trustees in deciphering unkempt financial records, thereby reducing the estate's value and prolonging the nightmare for the surviving loved ones. One uncomfortable talk can spare you this situation.

> It costs $241,080 for a middle-income couple to raise a child from birth to 18 years.
> Source: U.S. Department of Agriculture 2011 report

Regarding children, it's guaranteed they will cost you money (and time). As important as emotional maturity is to being a good parent, financial preparedness is equally important. Save for parenthood just as you would any other goal. (Note: if your employer's attitude is that parental leave is a sabbatical, re-read the "Job Loss" and "Job Change" sections earlier in this chapter.) The IRS Child Tax Credit Worksheet determines whether you are eligible for a tax savings. The Uniform Transfers to Minors Act (UTMA) has also been promoted as a tax-saving measure by shifting investment income onto your child's tax return. There are disadvantages. For example, capital gains will have to be recognized at some point, and the funds are taxed at the parents' marginal tax rate. Also, the asset will be counted if your child seeks financial aid. You'll also lose custodial control over a UTMA when the child is 18 or 21. A better way to teach your child about savings and taxes may be when your child starts a part-time job (presuming the wages aren't destined for a college fund) to open a Roth IRA in the child's name for investing some of the child's income. If you can afford it, sponsor a matching program for every dollar the child invests. A $1,000 investment at 8 percent beginning at age 15 results in $815,000 by age 65—more than twice the amount of a worker who starts saving the same amount at 25. In the event you have difficulty severing the financial purse strings to your bundle of joy (or vice versa), avoid the mistake of sacrificing your financial stability to support older (physically and mentally capable) children. Forty-five percent of working parents have a child 25 or older whom they financially support. Worse, 38 percent are saving less for retirement because of it, and 29 percent are delaying retirement, according to a 2007 survey from research firm Putnam Investments and Brightwork Partners.

A final word about caregiving: pets. Furry or otherwise, they cost money (and time). As with everything financial, consider whether there's room in your budget (and schedule) to provide food, veterinary care, and petsitting services before committing.

OTHER EVENTS

Financial management bolsters good opportunities that come your way and can also soften the blows. Preparedness is key to enabling you to act when either occurs.

Becoming Your Own Boss

Sometimes there are rewards for not following the herd. Yet, it takes more than guts to strike out on your own; it takes financial building blocks, too. If your business development efforts have built you client receivables, don't think you can bank on immediate receipt of those receivables when you exit a firm to start your solo career. It's not uncommon for firms to pay out receivables to a departing attorney (especially a partner) over a number of years. Protect your financial health by paying off debt, maintaining the emergency fund, and maxing out retirement savings. Before your solo career thrives, it's important to your financial success that you have a sound financial net worth—both so you live comfortably and can obtain financing should you need it to run your operation. Otherwise, your practice will run you instead of you running your practice.

Buying a Second Home

A second home for vacation or eventual retirement conjures up idyllic images of a spacious beach house or ski lodge, with your fabulous friends driving up for the weekend, their black Range Rovers and Mercedes arriving on your manicured drive, lining up in rows like a box of chocolates. That beautiful retreat can turn into a House of Blues without understanding it is a full-time financial commitment. Depending on the property, your current mortgage, property taxes, insurance, and maintenance could likely all be doubled, so budget accordingly.

Becoming Widowed

Sadly, becoming widowed is not a status reserved only for old age. Following these tips can help alleviate the financial stresses during a time of grief. First, take two or three months off, allowing yourself time to grieve. Second, assess what your assets are and where they are, and define your goals and prepare a budget as discussed in Chapter 2. (If you haven't been the financial gatekeeper who has paid the bills and maintained the records, start learning now.) Finally, financial preparedness before a crisis occurs will ease anxiety and save you money. It's not enjoyable to contemplate, but if your significant other is diagnosed with a terminal illness or becomes a fatality in an accident, it's in your best interests to have as much done beforehand as possible. Have a financial conversation at least once a year, especially if you are not in charge of the family finances, so you know what you have and where it is (e.g., assets, bank accounts, insurance policies, and agents' phone numbers). Copious forms will require completion before money will be distributed from investments and insurance, yet bills will have to be paid and decisions made, such as whether to sell the home; handling family care and managing day-to-day liquidity will require attention, and having your records in order will help you get a solid footing.

ESTATE PLANNING

As an attorney, you know the consequences of not planning for the inevitable. Yet, statistically, there's a surprising number of attorneys who don't have the basic documents executed, presumably because they're pressed for time or they have difficulty coming to grips with their own mortality. In any event, make it easier on your loved ones and have the documents listed in the following box in order. Potential embarrassment should motivate you on this one: think of your mourners speculating about the wisdom of a lawyer who dies without a will!

ESSENTIAL INFORMATION BINDER

In a secure location and confidentially protected manner, maintain these documents in a binder and/or encrypted electronic folder of portable document format (pdf) and word processing files:

- Copy of completed financial institution's form(s) for IOLTA Access by Assisting Attorney;
- Power of Attorney Authorizing Assisting Attorney to run business, as needed, including IOLTA signatory;
- List of Passwords for computer system(s) and bank and other accounts;
- Up-to-Date Chart of All Files for Transitioning and Closure;
- Instructions for Loved Ones and Personal Representative of the Estate about the designated Assisting Attorney responsibilities;
- Designated Assisting Attorney and contact information;
- Updated list of Law Practice Contacts (e.g., Employees, Clients, Vendors, Suppliers, Memberships);
- Draft of Letter for Assisting Attorney to Provide Notification to Client(s) about Deceased Lawyer;
- Draft of Letter from Assisting Attorney to Client(s) Authorizing Release of Client File(s) to New Attorney;
- State Bar's Client File Retention Rules;
- If state law allows attorneys to sell their practices, include Instructions to Personal Representative, and Will Provisions Corresponding to the Duties Concerning the Closing and/or Selling of the Practice instructions.

Source: Susan A. Berson, "Death of a Practice: After Lawyer Dies, Her Friend Is Faced with Closing Down Her Firm," *ABA Journal Magazine* (January 2013).

Solo and small-firm practitioners should also include an essential information binder, zip drive, or thumbnail drive in their estate plans that contains sufficient operating authorizations and information for another attorney to handle the details of shutting down the firm—should the unthinkable happen—or of handling business if you become incapacitated.

At the very least, password knowledge is key for those who will have to take care of your office and handle clients' inquiries. Ensure that passwords to access your computers and accounts are provided in a secure location.

TAKE INVENTORY

(1) Wills, trusts (for children, pets), shared custody agreement (domestic partners)

(2) Health Care Proxy, Power of Attorney

(3) Bank, brokerage account, retirement statements

(4) Safety-deposit boxes—check whether sealed upon death and need to have a co-owner

(5) Insurance policies and agent contact information

(6) Tax returns

(7) Credit card and other debt information

(8) Locations of secured places (safe, safety-deposit box)

(9) E-mail accounts and passwords

(10) Property records for real estate, cars, and other major assets

(11) Solo and Small-Firm Essential Information Binder

Chapter 11

Giving Back

It is everyone's obligation to put back into the world at least the equivalent of what they take out of it.

—Albert Einstein

Many lawyers participate in the much-needed pro bono efforts involving everyday landlord/tenant matters and immigration issues as well as news-making wage disputes and memorable, headline-grabbing DNA exonerations. There are other creative ways for lawyers to give back, however. No matter how little you think you have, there is always someone who has it worse. For those with charity at heart, it's understood that donation of time and money is a privilege and an obligation to one's community. For others, donating can provide a tangible benefit in the form of charitable deductions on a tax return. Whatever your impetus, giving back to your community provides a happy return. Share your expertise, time, and money. Figure out what skill you have to offer and the cause to unite it with, then get started.

BUT, I HAVE NO MONEY

Maybe you don't, but you know how to use a phone, navigate the Internet, and pound the pavement. Fund-raising is always needed. You can send letters and e-mails—both from the comfort of your home or office—soliciting donations. If you're especially adept at raising money, consider starting a foundation. Many lawyers have started nonprofits to fill a void they saw in their communities. The Wills for Heroes Foundation began with a lawyer filling a local need to provide no-cost estate planning documents to emergency workers, and now, with the help of a second lawyer, it's gone national. The bottom line: if the community needs your help, you help. Don't be a cosmic ingrate.

> For New York lawyer Bari Zahn, creating LivingBeyondBelief.org had a personal impetus. She started the foundation in honor of her deceased uncle to educate high schoolers about HIV/AIDS and has received worldwide acclaim.

BUT, I HAVE NO TIME

Maybe you do. Volunteering can take as much or as little time as your schedule permits. There are thousands of organizations with varying needs and time commitments. Also, your effort need not be purely altruistic. You'll be getting back a return on your investment of time, though it will be intangible. For example, consider board membership as a résumé builder. Once a month, you lend your legal expertise and meet with other civic-minded and community-oriented people by serving on a nonprofit's board. It can also boost your presence with an employer when an organization is entrusting you with its future—encouraging the employer to trust you with additional responsibility.

Or, how about a quick cure for a bad day? Instead of diving into a pint of Haagen Dazs, a fifth of scotch, or [insert your poison here], try taking a 30-minute break to help someone. Add in another 30 minutes for your commute time, and before you respond, "I don't even have 30 minutes to spare, let alone 60," consider that you'd likely spend at least 30 minutes buying and consuming your poison, and another 30 minutes venting to someone in your trusted circle by whining or complaining about your problem without developing a resolution.

> By day, Bernie Knight is an award winning D.C. attorney, but, he's made time to put his Masters of Psychology degree to work. By providing counsel at a local shelter to help the homeless get back on their feet, Bernie is an example that a mere one-hour contribution can make a life-long difference in someone else's world."

It doesn't have to be an earth-shattering, time-consuming effort: man a hotline or the soup kitchen's food service line; read, draw, or play soccer or kickball at an after-school program; or assist with Senior's Taekwondo at a senior center. Prefer to keep face-time at the office? Help a starving artist analyze a royalty contract. If you prefer to take a stroll and think about your problems, stop by the animal shelter and check out a dog for a walk. You can think and walk at the same time, can't you? Aside from the temporary reprieve a volunteer-break will give you, you'll likely get a pick-me-up and gain a new perspective on your problem after helping someone out with hers.

Volunteering can also keep you young. A study by Community Service Volunteers (CSV) found volunteering had improved health, confidence, sense of purpose, and self-development for their study subjects. Need more evidence? Consider a report from the Yale School of Public Health that maintaining positive thoughts and actions can keep you young. What better exercise than volunteering—making a positive contribution to someone or something else—to help you maintain those positive thoughts.

GET INSPIRED

Don't let a big "but" stop you from making a difference. You don't have to go it alone. It can be a firm-wide effort. Organize your colleagues and build a family a Habitat for Humanity home, or walk, run, and trot in a charity marathon. Some firms have their own charitable foundations and fund employee-driven community projects. Get involved.

No one expects you to stand around and sing "Kumbaya," but if you've been given good fortune, you've got to share it. The legacy we leave is how we live our lives every day. Right now, your good fortune may take the form of intelligence, opportunities, money, or all three. Show your appreciation for what you have by sharing it. Always remember, life is a series of choices. You can choose to be a good example of benevolence, generosity, and goodwill, or a horrible warning of arrogance, gluttony, and greed. Choose wisely.

Appendix A

Resources

CHAPTER ONE

Bankrate.com offers bank account comparisons at http://www.bankrate.com/checking.aspx

Tobias, Andrew. *The Only* Other *Investment Guide You'll Ever Need*. Simon & Schuster, 1987.

CHAPTER TWO

Berson, Susan A. "A Comfortable Retirement Requires Savvy Financial Housekeeping." *ABA Journal Magazine* (February 2014). http://www.abajournal.com/magazine/article/a_comfortable_retirement_requires_savvy_financial_housekeeping/.

Intuit: http://www.intuit.com (Quicken software, also available at office supply stores and Amazon.com; depending on the version purchased, priced around $30, after rebates)

Inflation History and Predictions

U.S. Department of Labor, Bureau of Labor Statistics: http://www.bls.gov

Congressional Budget Office: http://www.cbo.gov

Personal Finance

Women's Institute for Financial Education: http://www.wife.org (personal finance tips)

The Dollar Stretcher.com: http://www.stretcher.com (how to stretch a dollar)

Bills.com: http://www.bills.com/ways-to-save/ (online calculator to analyze expense saved with particular item)

Occupational Outlook Handbook: http://www.bls.gov (Bureau of Labor Statistics publication that details salaries in different occupations)

Homefair: http://www.homefair.com (offers a cost of living calculator for learning how much you'd need to earn to move to a new city in comparison with your current salary/city)

Darlin, Damon. "More Advice Graduates Don't Want to Hear." *New York Times*, June 2, 2007. http://www.nytimes.com.

Budget Vacations

http://www.priceline.com (travel reservations and information, such as 50 cities for $50 or less)

Lastminutetravel: http://www.lastminutetravel.com (lists spur-of-the-moment deals for hotels and airfare)

CHAPTER THREE

For additional information that may be of assistance regarding student loans, check the following websites:

U.S. Department of Education, Federal Student Aid: https://studentaid.ed.gov/repay-loans/understand/plans/ (summarizes benefits of payment options)

MYEDDEBT.com: https://www.myeddebt.com/borrower/ (U.S. Department of Education, Debt Resolution: Federal Student Aid)

Direct Loans: The William D. Ford Federal Direct Loan Program: http://www2.ed.gov/offices/OSFAP/DirectLoan/

National Consumer Law Center: http://www.nclc.org/

Bankruptcy

For a factual pattern where the appellate court affirmed the bankruptcy court's discharge of student loans, see *In Re:* Jeri Lynn Lee, Debtor. Jeri Lynn Lee, Plaintiff-Appellees v. Regions Bank Student Loans, Defendant-Appellant, Case 06-6049 (8th BAP 9/26/06); compare Rose v. U.S. Dep't of Ed. (*In re Rose*), 187 F. 926 (8th Cir. 1999)

IRS: http://www.irs.gov (Topic 456—Student Loan Interest Deduction)

Berson, Susan A. "Get a Handle on Student Loan Debt." *ABA Journal Magazine* (May 2013). http://www.abajournal.com/magazine/article/get_a_handle_on_student_loan_debt/.

Federal Revenue Bank of New York, "Student Loan Debt by Age Group": http://www.newyorkfed.org/studentloandebt/

"Private Student Loans," Report to the Senate Committee on Banking, Housing, and Urban Affairs, the Senate Committee on Health, Education, Labor, and Pensions, the House of Representatives Committee on Financial Services, and the House of Representatives Committee on Education and the Workforce, Consumer Financial Protection Bureau (August 29, 2012): http://files.consumerfinance.gov/f/201207_cfpb_Reports_Private-Student-Loans.pdf

CHAPTER FOUR

www.leadfusion.com (offers a calculator to help choose the best credit card)

Financialcalculators.com: http://www.fincalc.com/ (financial calculators)

Tips on how to prevent identity theft, and what can be done if you're a victim, can be found at http://www.consumer.gov, http://www.ftc.gov/, and https://www.privacyrights.org/

Secret History of the Credit Card: http://www.pbs.org/wgbh/pages/frontline/shows/credit/

Individual Credit Reporting Bureaus

Equifax: http://www.equifax.com/home/en_us, 1-800-685-1111

Experian: https://www.experian.com/, 1-866-200-6020

TransUnion: http://www.transunion.com/, 1-800-888-4213

freecreditreport.com (provides you with a "free" credit report and credit score, yet enrolls you in a "trial membership" for its credit monitoring service; if you don't cancel the trial within 30 days, a $12.95 monthly fee will be incurred)

AnnualCreditReport.com (sponsored by the three major credit bureaus—Equifax, Experian, and TransUnion; provides you with one free credit report [but not your credit score] from each credit bureau over a period of 12 months)

For More Information on Credit Repair Scams

Better Business Bureau: http://www.bbb.org

National Association of Attorneys General: http://www.naag.org (click on your state's attorney general)

http://www.consumerworld.org

Bankruptcy scenario: Consider *In re* Aprea (Bkrtcy. E.D. Tex. May 18, 2007) (Chapter 13 debtor did not propose plan in good faith, requiring dismissal. He used unsecured credit to finance his living expenses prior to bankruptcy, anticipated spending more than $700 per month on food and recreation, leased a new luxury vehicle for his fiancée, then proposed to pay one unsecured creditor for his 50-inch TV and surround-sound system but pay only 0.005 percent of his remaining unsecured debt.)

For Car Purchases

http://www.carbuyingtips.com (car buying tips)

http://www.carinfo.com (car tips)

http://www.consumerreports.org (offers various tips on purchasing cars and other consumer items)

http://www.kbb.com (Kelley Blue Book valuations)

http://www.edmunds.com (guide to what types of cars/models retain their value)

CHAPTER FIVE

U.S. Department of Housing and Urban Development: http://portal.hud.gov/hudportal/HUD (offers info on buying a home and on buying programs in your state)

Mortgage calculators: http://money.cnn.com; www.bankrate.com; www.quicken.com; http://www.mortgage101.com; http://www.realtor.com; www.priceline.com

For a printable/downloadable worksheet of questions to ask mortgage lenders, go to www.bankrate.com and enter "Work sheet: interviewing mortgage lenders" in the search box

Federal Reserve Board, "Consumer Handbook on Adjustable Rate Mortgages," http://www.federalreserve.gov/pubs/brochure.htm

Mortgage Bankers Association, "How to Shop for a Mortgage," http://www.mbaa.org

Home Inspections

National Association of Home Inspectors: http://www.nahi.org

Bankruptcy and the danger of buying more home than you need or can afford: *In re* Loper (Bkrtcy D. Colo. May 18, 2007) (Chapter 13 debtors failed to establish that retention of their home, with its associated expense, was reasonably necessary. Thus, confirmation of their plan was not warranted, despite debtors' contention that their home was one of the least expensive in the area. The debtors were spending $5,690 per month on a home in which they had little or no equity. The housing costs devoured two-thirds of their monthly net income. The plan provided for payment of less than 10 percent of their unsecured debt.)

CHAPTER SIX

http://www.communicatingforamerica.org/ (a list of states with risk pools for health insurance)

http://www.ambest.com, https://www.moodys.com, http://www.standardandpoors.com (Check the insurance company's ratings on these websites. Stick with A rated to ensure that you have a company that can pay your disability claims.)

"Health Wealth: Retirement Planning Includes Caring for Yourself." *ABA Journal Magazine* (April 2014).

http://www.insure.com (provides quotes for travel insurance)

Social Security: http://www.ssa.gov/disability (disability insurance information)

Northwestern Mutual Financial Network: www.nwmf.com (disability policies)

Berson, Susan A. "Get a Plan B: Disability Insurance Needs to Be in Your Insurance Plan." *ABA Journal Magazine* (June 2011). http://www.abajournal.com/magazine/article/get_a_plan_b_disabiility_insurance/

For Health Care Power of Attorney Forms

University of Michigan Health System: http://www.med.umich.edu/1libr/aha/umlegal02.htm (sample Health Care POA form)

Family Caregivers Online: http://www.familycaregiversonline.net/legal-resources (sample POA forms for all states)

National Center for Lesbian Rights: http://www.nclrights.org (offers Health Care POA info

CHAPTER SEVEN

Schwed, Fred. *Where Are the Customers' Yachts? or, A Good, Hard Look at Wall Street.* Wiley Investment Classics, 1940.

Graham, Benjamin. *The Intelligent Investor.* 1973, Rev. Ed. 2003.

Blodget, Henry. *The Wall Street Self-Defense Manual.*

"Warren Buffett on the Stock Market," *Fortune* (December 10, 2001).

Ody, Elizabeth. "How to Evaluate ETF's." Kiplinger (August 2010). http://www.kiplinger.com/article/investing/T022-C000-S002-how-to-evaluate-etfs.html.

Bajaj, Vikas. "Bear Stearns to Bail Out Troubled Fund." *New York Times*, June 23, 2007. www.nyt.com.

Norris, Floyd. "Wells Fargo Fined in Disclosure Case." *New York Times*, June 27, 2007. www.nyt.com.

http://www.morningstar.com (research investments)

The Motley Fool: http://www.fool.com (contrary view of investing trends, mutual funds, stocks)

The Street: http://www.thestreet.com (in-depth look at what mutual fund managers are buying)

Dow Jones: http://new.dowjones.com (quotes, abstracts of analysts' research reports)

American Association of Individual Investors: http://www.aaii.com (information on investments, diversification, building portfolios)

Vanguard's Asset Allocation Calculator and Questionnaire: https://personal.vanguard.com/us/FundsInvQuestionnaire

Wells Fargo's Asset Allocation Calculator and Questionnaire: http://www.wellsfargoadvantagefunds.com/wfweb/wf/education/tools/asset.jsp

For Index Fund Accounts

Vanguard: www.vanguard.com

Fidelity: www.fidelity.com

Other Sources to Find a Mutual Fund

Kiplinger: http://www.kiplinger.com/article/investing (annually publishes rankings of best mutual funds)

www.fundfocus.com

www.quicken.com/investments/mutualfunds/finder

National Association of Personal Financial Advisors (NAPFA): http://www.napfa.org/ (to find a fee-only financial planner in your area, consult this website; also has helpful periodicals)

Wealthfront.com (online investment advice; your risk tolerance is determined via software, a financial plan is created, and no fee is charged up to $25,000 invested)

The Garrett Planning Network: http://garrettplanningnetwork.com (offers more than 300 certified financial planners charging fees from $180 to $240 per hour for in-person meetings; best for investors needing an initial planning session with minimal follow-up)

http://www.savingsbond.com (links for purchasing savings bonds)

AARP: http://www.aarp.org/ws/retirement-help-tools-old/

Center for Retirement Research at Boston College: http://crr.bc.edu/special-projects/interactive-tools/target-your-retirement/ (interactive tools for targeting retirement savings goals)

Fidelity's IRA Contribution Calculator: https://scs.fidelity.com/products/mobile/ira/ira-calc.shtml

Fidelity's Retirement Calculators and Tools: https://www.fidelity.com/calculators-tools/retirement/overview

T. Rowe Price, "Ready-2-Retire" tool: http://individual.troweprice.com/public/Retail/Retirement/Retirement-Planning/Nearing-Retirement

Vanguard's Retirement Calculator: https://retirementplans.vanguard.com/VGApp/pe/pubeducation/calculators/RetirementIncomeCalc.jsf

Bankrate.com: http://www.bankrate.com/calculators/retirement/retirement-plan-income-calculator.aspx

ES Planner: http://www.esplanner.com (basic option is currently free; it focuses on what you need to know about spending, rates of return, and Social Security benefits for purposes of maintaining the same standard of living during retirement)

Social Security Administration: https://secure.ssa.gov/acu/ACU_KBA/main.jsp?URL=/apps8z/ARPI/main.jsp?locale=en&LVL=4

"A Separate Consumer Price Index for the Elderly?" January 20, 2010 Congressional Research Services (CRS) Report for Congress, http://www.aging.senate.gov/crs/aging9.pdf.

Berson, Susan A. "Road to Retirement: Ways to Make Retirement Anything but Resignation." *ABA Journal Magazine* (January 2014). http://www.abajournal.com/magazine/article/road_to_retirement.

Berson, Susan A. "Don't Panic, Plan: Regular Saving and Asset Allocation Help Build a Retirement." *ABA Journal Magazine* (March 2014). http://www.abajournal.com/magazine/article/regular_saving_and_asset_allocation_help_build_a_retirement/.

Berson, Susan A. "Some Basic Rules for Using 'Bitcoin' as Virtual Money." *ABA Journal Magazine* (July 2013). http://www.abajournal.com/magazine/article/some_basic_rules_for_using_bitcoin_as_virtual_money/.

Berson, Susan A. "Bitcoin and Taxes" (June 2013). https://itunes.apple.com/us/book/bitcoins-and-taxes/id663529210?mt=11.

CHAPTER EIGHT

United States v. Windsor, 133 S. Ct. 2675 (2013) (U.S. Supreme Court found Section 3 of the Defense of Marriage Act to be unconstitutional, affording recognition of same-sex marriages)

IRS: IR-2013-72: "Treasury and IRS Announce That All Legal Same-Sex Marriages Will Be Recognized for Federal Tax Purposes; Ruling Provides Certainty, Benefits and Protections Under Federal Tax Law for Same-Sex Married Couples" (August 29, 2013).

IRS Notice 2013-61 (September 23, 2013) (provides guidance for employers and employees to claim refunds or adjust overpayments of FICA taxes and employment taxes with respect to certain benefits and remunerations provided to same-sex spouses)

National Conference of State Legislatures: http://www.ncsl.org/research/human-services/same-sex-marriage-laws.aspx (maintains updates concerning applicable legislative actions, including same-sex marriage laws)

www.irs.gov (enter "Tax Scams—How to Recognize and Avoid Them" in the search tool)

https://www.turbotax.com (offers tax prep software)

Tax Preparation Books

Ernst & Young publishes tax prep. book annually for the Form 1040

PriceWaterhouseCoopers publishes tax prep. book annually for the Form 1040

Berson, Susan A. *Federal Tax Litigation.* Law Journal Press, 2001.

Berson, Susan A. "Ask Questions, Look for IRS Red Flags Before Investing in Tax Shelters." *Kansas City Business Journal,* April 7, 2006.

Berson, Susan A. "IRS Collections Are Not Put Off by Offshore Assets." *Practical Tax Strategies* (December 1999).

CHAPTER NINE

Berson, Susan A. "Road to Retirement: Ways to Make Retirement Anything but Resignation." *ABA Journal Magazine* (January 2014). http://www.abajournal.com/magazine/article/road_to_retirement.

Savings/Retirement

To help you get a better idea of how much money you need, you can go to http://www.choosetosave.org and use the Employee Benefit Research Institute's free Ballpark E$timate worksheet.

https://www.livingto100.com (calculate when you might check out so you can help gauge how much money you'll need to live and also determine how to better your health)

http://www.bloomberg.com/invest/calculators/retire (retirement calculator)

http://money.cnn.com/calculator/retirement/retirement-need/ (retirement calculator)

Lee, Marlena I. "The Retirement Income Equation: Understanding How to Arrive at a Target Replacement Rate." *DC Dimensions* (Summer 2012). http://www.dfaus.com/pdf/dc_dimensions/2012summer/RetirementIncome_Summer2012.pdf (explains the framework about replacement rate targets and related research).

Low-Cost Index Funds

Vanguard: The Vanguard Extended Market Index fund (VEXMX) gives exposure to both large cap and small cap companies, across a wide variety of industries. The Vanguard Total International Stock Index fund (VGTSX) gives international exposure. An initial $3,000 investment in the VGTSX funds is required, so given the typical $4,000 annual IRA max, you may need to focus on the broad U.S. VEXMX fund first, and then add on the international fund in a future year.

T. Rowe Price funds: For a lower monthly or quarterly investment, it allows periodic investments of as low as $50. It has a low-cost, U.S.-based extended market index fund (PEXMX), as well as an international index fund (PIEQX).

http://www.retirementplanner.org

http://www.socialsecurity.gov

Medicare: http://www.cms.gov (trustee's report dated April 23, 2007: Social Security paying out more in benefits than it collects in payroll taxes starting in 2017)

www.ssa.gov (Should the government radically fix the siphon on the Social Security system, you can visit the Social Security Administration website's planner and calculator section for factors that influence the benefits received.)

Updegrave, Walter. "Build the Big Sum You'll Need." *Money Magazine*. http://money.cnn.com/2007/03/09/magazines/moneymag/retireearly_savings.moneymag.

Updegrave, Walter. "Fill Your Riskiest Gap: Insurance." *Money Magazine*. http://money.cnn.com/2007/03/09/magazines/moneymag.

Tebo, Margaret Graham. "Retired, Then Re-Energized." *ABA Journal* (April 2007). http://www.abajournal.com/magazine/article/retired_then_re_energized1/.

CHAPTER TEN

Aaron, Deborah. *What Can You Do with a Law Degree.* Niche Press.
http://www.newlywedfinances.com
"For the Public Good." http://www.workingmother.com/content/public-good
http://www.workingmother.com/content/2013-working-mother-and-flex-time-lawyers-best-law-firms-women (list of best law firms for women)
Fortune 100 Best Companies to Work For 2011 (four law firms that offer sabbaticals made the list)
Family Caregiver Alliance: https://caregiver.org; 415-434-3388 (offers information for caregiver concerns; newsletters in English, Spanish, and Chinese; and an online support group)
National Alliance for Caregiving: http://www.caregiving.org; 301-718-8444 (a national resource center that provides information on elder-care conferences, books, and training for professionals)
National Association of Area Agencies on Aging: http://www.n4a.org, 202-872-0888 (an advocacy group for local aging agencies; offers The Eldercare Locator, 1-800-677-1116, http://www.eldercare.gov, a service that provides local resource and referral organizations, which, in turn, recommend home health care aides)
American Association of Homes and Services for the Aging: www.aahsa.org, 202-783-2242 (publishes free brochure on how to choose nursing home or assisted living facilities, a directory of continuing-care retirement communities, and information on long-term care insurance)
"Lessons of the Am Law 100," *American Lawyer* (May 2007).
www.flextimelawyers.com (matches lawyers with short-term projects)
Rozhon, Tracie. "The Tyranny of the 2nd Home." *New York Times,* May 18, 2007. http://www.nytimes.com.
Berson, Susan A. "Death of a Practice: After Lawyer Dies, Her Friend Is Faced with Closing Down Her Firm." *ABA Journal Magazine* (January 2013). http://www.abajournal.com/magazine/article/death_of_a_practice_terminally_ill_lawyers_friend_faces_closing_down_firm/

"Planning Ahead: A Guide to Protecting Your Clients' Interests in the Event of Your Disability or Death." Oregon Bar Association, Professional Liability Fund.

"Checklist for Lawyers Planning to Protect Clients' Interests in the Event of the Lawyer's Death, Disability, Impairment, or Incapacity." http://www.osbplf.org/docs/aids/Cklist%20Lawyers%20PlantoProtect.pdf

"Succession Planning." Washington State Bar Association. http://www.wsba.org/Resources-and-Services/Ethics/Succession-Planning (online form letters and agreements).

CHAPTER ELEVEN

http://www.charitywatch.org/ (rates charities)

www.irs.gov (lists legitimate tax-exempt charities and not-for-profits)

Nawrocki, Jill. "An Unusual Rep: Firms Compete to Win Pro Bono Projects." *American Lawyer* (March 2007).

"Volunteering Keeps You Young." BBC News, December 8, 2004. http://news.bbc.co.uk.

Filisko, G. M. "Many Happy Returns." *ABA Journal* (April 2007).

Mathis, Karen J. "Liberty Under Law." *ABA Journal* (May 2007) (discusses ABA Youth at Risk Initiative).

Levy, Becca. 2007 Bottom Line Health Newsletter. Yale School of Public Health.

Appendix B

Spender Quiz: What Kind of Spender Are You?

The following questions are designed to provide an illuminating snapshot of the emotions and thought processes that may drive your buying decisions. Circle the answer that applies.

You're going grocery shopping. You:

(1) have a list that you stick closely to of items to purchase based on a look in your frig and cupboards;

(2) have no list, but a general idea of what you need to buy;

(3) buy what looks appealing.

Waiting in line at the grocery store, you:

(1) browse the magazines, but don't buy them;

(2) grab one or two things, but not completely load up the tab;

(3) load up on magazines, candy, whatever you see that you may want.

Your friend begs you to go shopping. You don't need anything, but you go and:

(1) purchase nothing, even though you see something that you want, because you'd rather allocate your money toward your goals and the "want" is not one of them;

(2) purchase whatever you want so long as it doesn't break your bank account;

(3) purchase whatever catches your eye regardless of whether you truly need it, and if you don't have the cash to cover it, you know that you can charge it because you have an available balance.

Your microwave broke. You:

(1) get on the Internet and research the prices and models at the stores in your area to find one you like that fits within your budget;

(2) go to a store where you normally have received good deals, look around, and buy the one you like;

(3) go to the first store you see that sells microwaves and buy one.

It's payday at work, and the money is direct-deposited into your account. The first thing you do is:

(1) plan the expenses for the next couple of weeks to figure out what needs to be paid and what can be put in the emergency fund or savings;

(2) relax, knowing that you'll figure out what to do with the money later;

(3) celebrate by treating yourself to something new like the new arrival your favorite store just e-mailed you about that you find appealing.

You've been thinking about getting a dog. You:

(1) research the types of breeds, their temperaments, and requirements that would be best suited to your money, temperament, and time constraints, then get on the Internet and research animal shelters in your area for animals that are available for adoption before actually deciding whether a dog is the right fit for you at this time;

(2) have an idea of what you can afford and the type of breed you want, so you adopt one without any further research;

(3) buy the most expensive pup you like from a breeder because that means it's the healthiest.

Your secretary has been telling you how much she and her recently unemployed husband love their new big-screen TV they bought with a financing offer of no payments until next year. You've been wanting a big screen, so you:

(1) research what is the best quality big screen and the prices, determine that you don't have enough saved for that yet, and continue saving, putting off the purchase until you can pay cash for it;

(2) buy the cheapest big screen that fits within your savings, even though the salesperson provides you with a credible report that shows it won't last more than two years;

(3) decide that if your secretary and her unemployed husband can afford it, so can you, and finance the big screen.

It's summer, the air conditioner has broken, and you have to replace it because you're living in Nevada where it's 110 in the shade. You drain the emergency fund to pay for it, and now your friend wants to go out to dinner at a wonderful French restaurant. You:

(1) are tempted and explain you'd love to go with her, but will have to pass because you don't have any disposable income to spare after replacing the a/c. She brings over a bottle of wine and you cook whatever is in the fridge;

(2) invite her over for dinner, picking up a couple of yummy things at the grocery store, and eat-in at half the price of the restaurant;

(3) accept, figuring you'll order something cheap, and if the restaurant she's chosen is going to cost you more than $20 to $30, you'll just charge it.

When you receive your credit card bill, you:

(1) pay the full amount because you don't purchase anything unless you will have the cash to cover it at the end of the month when the bill comes;

(2) pay back more than the minimum, but not enough to pay it off because you can't afford other living expenses if you do;

(3) pay the minimum so you can have more cash to play with during the next couple of weeks.

You just arrived home after buying a $30 item from a store 30 minutes away to learn it doesn't work. You:

(1) immediately return it, or schedule time tomorrow to do so, and get your money back;

(2) put it aside, deciding you'll return it the next time you're near the store. Then, you forget about it, and when you remember, it's too late so you settle for a store credit;

(3) decide to forget about returning it. It's not worth the hassle for $30.

When you hear someone talk about money, you:

(1) have enough to pay living expenses and your savings account, and think that as long as you carefully watch what you spend your paycheck on, you'll be okay;

(2) become a bit tense because while you're meeting your living expenses, you're unable to save consistently, and wish you had more in the emergency fund;

(3) complain that you never have enough even after you received a raise.

When you shop, you:

(1) buy things when you need them, prepare lists ahead of time, and try to remember to ask yourself whether what you are considering is something you really need versus something you just want;

(2) buy things that you want and need, but only if you can afford it;

(3) buy things with the motto, "I'm in the hole so deep, what does a few more dollars matter" or "life is short—if you want it, buy it."

In general, when you have a big purchase, you think:

(1) I'll start researching for the best quality and price;

(2) forget research because it's all a wash;

(3) who needs research, money matters are boring and I'm swamped. I'd rather spend my free time on a more exciting outlet.

You need a suit for a meeting with clients. At the store, you find a quality suit, though the price is a bit over your price range, but it is made to last. So you:

(1) buy it, pledging to reallocate money from another category in your budget, such as your monthly latte fund, to cover the cost;

(2) opt to buy two cheaper suits for the price of the one suit, because even though the material is cheaper on the two cheap suits, you'll add two new suits to your closet instead of just the one. Plus, since they're so cheap, you can always buy more suits when the fabric gives out;

(3) leave it hanging on the rack because if it doesn't have the highly coveted designer label, and Hollywood isn't wearing it, you're not buying it. So, you pay the extra money to special order something, knowing that it will be out of style by year's end.

ADD UP THE NUMBER OF "1", "2," and "3" ANSWERS
TOTALS: _____1 _____2 ______3

MOSTLY 1s: Investment Shopper—Generally, you're a smart shopper. You don't fall for the bells and whistles that are unneeded, and you don't buy cheap things that won't last. Things that have stood the test of time hold the greatest interest. You're in a place where you can truly appreciate quality over flash and fads. Let other people fall for the disposable, mass-produced look—you're too unique. Once you have a clear vision of what you want, you make a plan to get there. You likely break down big goals into smaller steps that make them feel more attainable. With each small step completed, you feel the satisfaction of accomplishment, and it helps maintain your motivation to stay on budget and move toward accomplishing your financial goals.

MOSTLY 2s: Impulse Shopper—You may understand that it's possible to look hot without melting your credit cards; however, even though you may only charge small amounts, or withdraw small amounts of cash, your money seems to leak out of your pocket almost instantly. When money is in your wallet, or in your bank account, you feel either compelled to spend it, or are fine with spending it. Psychological studies suggest that many impulse shoppers range from frustrated, "creative" types who have imaginations that can fuel their shopping sprees to individuals with low self-esteem who may feel that they do not deserve to be prosperous. When you hand over your cash, you are handing over responsibility for your life or decision making. Still doesn't sound like you? Then maybe you are the deprived child. If treats were the cure for blue days, or if you were deprived as a child and always dreamed of getting yourself the reasonable things you were denied, you could be associating the purchase of inconsequential nothings with feeling good. Unfortunately, that good feeling likely ends when you look at your bank account balance. The good news is that although impulse shoppers may dig themselves into debt, they can recover. Try viewing the process of getting out of debt and managing money as a challenge, and use your creativity to find more satisfying ways to fill yourself up than mini-shopping sprees. Extending your creative ways to your financial world will give amazing results. If you can start to see saving your money as a challenge, then you may have fun finding creative ways to do so, and it can help you become more materially comfortable. Otherwise, being in debt for you will be like having a large ship steered by a very small rudder. You're staying afloat and moving, but not going very fast and not getting very far ahead. If it helps to equate getting out of debt and building a savings program to accomplishing a work project, treat it like a challenging document production or due diligence task. Initially the mountains of documents and electronic information can be overwhelming, but when you break it down into smaller steps, completing the project becomes more attainable. Break your debt down into small pay-offs, or your savings program into small deposits. With each small step completed, you feel the satisfaction of accomplishment. As you break your debt down into small pay-offs, while building your savings up each month, with each small step completed, you'll feel confident and motivated to continue becoming debt-free and build your wealth.

MOSTLY 3s: Emotional or Vanity Spender—You're using retail therapy to fill a void. "I deserve to treat myself" or "If I only had that, my life would be better" are the classic lines. Whether it's insecurity, acceptance, anxiety, or loneliness, the sooner you realize that money can't buy you a sense of peace for any of these feelings, the sooner you'll be able to become debt-free and financially stable and build wealth. Until then, you'll continue to use credit cards to supplement your income, regardless of whether you're earning $60,000 or $1 million, and you'll never get to where you need to be for financial success. Your purchases are largely the creation of vanity, rather than a logical need. Money can't buy love, or so goes the song. But, it also can't buy true respect or acceptance. Psychological studies suggest that emotional shoppers tend to search for these intangibles with the tangible. Splurges may be triggered by insecurity or guilt, with the true motivation being reassurance. When you don't feel validated at work or home, if your first thought is to buy something to make yourself feel better, in lieu of spending, try substituting something else that normally makes you happy. Some emotional shoppers may also have a tendency toward the "Daddy Warbuck's attitude," meaning price is no obstacle when it comes to my friends or family. Just because your love may be equivalent to Cartier doesn't mean that you have to break your bank account to buy a gift there, especially when you're charging it and won't have the cash to cover it when the statement arrives. Nor does it mean that the expensive gift will guarantee the return of true feelings toward you. For you, dealing with debt and risk is like anything else in life—you have to know where the line is that you won't cross, because there's always going to be someone bringing out some emotion that is ready to push you over that line, and if you haven't decided where your line is, you're going to get yourself in serious financial trouble.

For all types of shoppers, a good software program can revolutionize and streamline your budget planning to help you stay on track and achieve your financial goals.

Appendix C

Financial To-Do Checklist

(1) Determine financial goals ("If you fail to plan, you plan to fail.").

- ☐ Short-term (within a year)
- ☐ Medium-term (1–5 years)
- ☐ Long-term (over 5 years)

(2) Establish a record-keeping system, and destroy discarded receipts/statements.

(3) Budget: Take 10 percent off your monthly take-home pay before developing a budget to meet necessary expenses.
Apply the 10 percent to maxing out your retirement contribution and establishing an emergency savings fund, unless credit card and student loan debt exists. If debt exists, pay off credit cards. If your employer has a matching retirement program, budget so you can participate in it, and pay off credit card(s). Analyze student loan debt options, along with computing interest rate and tax deduction to determine whether pay-off is appropriate. Once credit cards are paid off, after your paycheck is direct-deposited, have 10 percent directly routed from your checking account monthly toward: (i) maxing out the annual retirement contribution; and (ii) emergency savings equal to six months' pay. Maintain the emergency fund in an interest-bearing, federally insured account. When the credit card debt is paid off, and (i) and (ii) have been accomplished, allocate funds toward an investment account or other goals, such as making a down payment for a home or purchasing a car.

(4) Credit Cards: know interest rate and pay off balances monthly

(5) Car: if financed, accelerate payments on debt to eliminate interest being paid to creditor instead of your goals

(6) Home Loan: consider (i) shortest term; (ii) 20 percent down payment; and (iii) if you are buying five years from now, put money in certificates of deposit or short-term bond fund for maximum interest earned.

(7) Insurance: protect your assets, including your ability to earn income

(8) Investments: (i) diversify; (ii) maintain low costs and taxes; (iii) no-load index funds offer the broadest diversification, and if you can invest monthly, market fluctuations will matter less to long-term growth. The indexes are: Wilshire 5000 Index (large, mid, and small cap U.S.), S&P 500 Index (large cap U.S.), Russell 2000 (small cap U.S.), MISC EAFE (broad international stock index), Lehmann Aggregate Bond Index (broad U.S. bond index); (iv) allocate money in a combination of U.S. stock funds, international stock funds, and U.S. bond funds. Make certain that U.S. stock funds have a mix of large cap, medium cap, and small cap stocks. Also, make sure that U.S. stock funds have a mix of value stocks and growth stocks.

(9) Conduct annual review of net worth, credit report, and diversification allocations.

Index

E

F